AuDHD &

Growing up Distracted

Laura G.A

First published 2023

Editing assistance by Patrick Fagan Copyright © Laura A., 2023

ISBN: 9798856191959

Imprint: Independently published All rights reserved.

This publication is designed to provide accurate and authoritative information concerning the subject matter covered.

This publication is meant as a source of information for the reader, however, it is not meant as a substitute for direct expert experience. If such a level of assistance is required, the services of a competent professional should be sought.

All that is gold does not glitter,

Not all those who wander are lost.

The old that is strong does not wither,

Deep roots are not reached by the frost.

From the ashes, a fire shall be woken,

A light from the shadows shall spring.

Renewed shall be the blade that was broken,

The crownless again shall be king.

——J.R.R. Tolkien, The Fellowship of the Ring

Prologue

This book has been burning in the recesses of my mind, eager to see the light ever since I found out I had ADHD. I was initially nervous to take that leap at first, but then one day I just felt a surge of inspiration and just started writing. And I haven't stopped. That's why I'm here in my bed with my glasses held together by tape, thinking how ironic it is, to delay getting them fixed, right after an ADHD diagnosis and writing this book (The Joys of Procrastination).

First, While the official diagnosis is Autism Spectrum Disorder, I felt more comfortable with the title of Autism. So, I will jump between Autism or Autistic person/individual for much of this book. I do use ASD for more clinical information, I hope this does not become too irritating or confusing.

Second, let me tell you, this is not a self-help book, this is a self-discovery book. It's a book about this journey I've embarked on. And maybe by sharing my journey, and the little nuggets of wisdom I've picked up along the way, can help others. Or at least give them hope that there are answers, and spark that a-ha, Eureka moment.

... Third, I'm an animal behaviour researcher (in training), not a psychiatrist, so I'm not qualified to give advice, I can only tell my story and use the research available. I can only offer my perspective, with a touch of background information from current research, which I will cite at the end of the book.

I had always drifted aimlessly through most of my life, feeling like something was off but not knowing what it was. I had a splendid assortment of labels: lazy, full of potential, lacking focus, making mistakes, needing to work harder, inappropriate, too quiet, too chatty, weird, odd, and eccentric. I sometimes found it difficult to grasp things that seemed so easy to others. Inside I was so determined, trying so hard but there was nothing to show for it. One day I finally asked WHY? That was the turning point for me. I asked that simple, yet crucial question.

After that day everything changed, I was diagnosed with ADHD, have an unofficial Autism diagnosis, waiting for the official diagnosis. Everything was starting to make sense; the puzzle pieces were fitting together. Before the official ADHD diagnosis, I listened to TedTalks from adults, and it was an immediate light-bulb moment. I had always felt different, out of place, and misunderstood. I had struggled with school, work, relationships, and emotions. I had tried so hard to fit in, to be normal, to please everyone. But nothing ever worked. I was always frustrated, restless, bored, anxious, and depressed. I hated myself for being this way. But when I learned that I had ADHD and Autism, I realized that I was not broken, defective, or crazy. I was just wired differently. I had a unique way of thinking, feeling, and experiencing the world. I had strengths and talents that others did not have. I had a lot to offer and a lot to learn.

With this revelation, I read and listened to everything I could get my hands on. I wanted to understand, not only what this diagnosis meant to me but why this diagnosis was so long coming. I read books, articles, blogs, podcasts anything I could find. Through podcasts and YouTube vlogs, I gathered a lot of information about the science behind ADHD and Autism, the symptoms, the treatments, and strategies. I learned about the history and the culture of neurodiversity, the challenges, and the opportunities. I learned about the differences between men and women with ADHD and Autism. How women tend to get diagnosed later in life after a history of being misdiagnosed or overlooked. I was not so lucky with books for a long time, I struggled to find good information and support in the literature on the topic. There were not many books out there that discussed ADHD and Autism in a clear, honest, and respectful way. Some of them were too dry and technical, while others were too biased and outdated. They didn't reflect the reality and diversity of people with ADHD and Autism. I decided to write this book to share my journey and the journeys of others going through life with ADHD, Autism and AuDHD with you. To show you how I went from feeling lost and hopeless to finding myself and my purpose. To inspire you to do the same if you are in a similar situation. To inform you about the facts and myths of ADHD and Autism. And to hopefully empower you to embrace your neurodiversity and celebrate your uniqueness.

This book aims to fill that gap and offer a fresh perspective. I hope that by sharing my story and the latest research, I can help others who are going on the same journey. Now I must admit between the time I first wrote this epilogue and the finishing of this book, new books have appeared, I hope to read them all and I have high hopes for the literature now out there.

I loved learning about the experiences of other people like me through their stories those who had gone through similar struggles and triumphs. I realized that I was not alone. There were millions of people out there who shared my diagnosis, my challenges, my passions. There were communities and networks of support.

This leads me to this book, in chapter 1, I begin with the

moment I got diagnosed with ADHD and autism. It will show you how this diagnosis changed my life. I will tell you what made me seek help, how it felt to finally have a name for what I was experiencing, and how it made me see myself in a new light. In Chapter 2, I will explain what ADHD and autism are, how they affect the brain and the behaviour of people who have them. How they are different for boys and girls, and why many girls go undiagnosed for a long time. Just a little warning I'll discuss research papers relating to ADHD and Autism (if you are not interested move on to chapter 4 which is straight to the memoir). Chapter 3 looks at all the definitions and backgrounds of the traits, comorbidities, and general terms associated with ADHD and Autism. Then we take a quick journey through my life, and how undiagnosed ADHD and Autism affected my childhood (Chapter 4). How I saw the world, and the traits of ADHD and Autism I grew up with, that are now so obvious. I'll discuss my sensory issues (smell, light, emotions) and my stims. I'll talk about my education (Chapter 5), the workplace (Chapter 6), relationships (Chapter 7), and Home and Family life (Chapter 8). Chapter 9 looks at how those with ADHD and Autism may be affected by medical issues. Chapter 10 discusses my official diagnosis and the different treatment methods available, including my own. Finally, chapter 11 consists of stories by others who have been diagnosed, how they live their lives, how they are affected, and whether they have found ways to cope.

I am going to be an open book (don't mind the pun) during this entirety. I'm going to be upfront, extremely honest, and admit some aspects of my life I've told nobody. Why? Shame, mostly, and I just didn't know how to open up or put words to how I felt. I've read back on this book now and I have that feeling that I most definitely overshared. But if you can relate, I can say my job is done here. Maybe you won't. That's ok too. Only by talking about these struggles, real change can be made.

ADHD and Autism can affect you in so many aspects of your lives, not just work or school. I hope that by reading this book, you will gain a better understanding of yourself or someone you know who has ADHD or Autism. This book is a message that you are not alone, there is a community, and if you find yourself on this journey, we will welcome you with open arms. You are never too old for a diagnosis, it can change your life, and everyone deserves answers. I hope that you will feel less alone, less ashamed, and less confused. I hope that you will feel more confident, more curious, and more hopeful by the end.

AuDHD & Me

I hope that you will join me on this adventure of
discovering the wonders of neurodiversity.

Contents

Chapter 1
Let's not start at the very beginning!

This journey started unpredictably on 01/11/2022, four days after I celebrated my 33rd Birthday (I would later find out that getting a diagnosis in the late twenties or early thirties is not unusual for women with ADHD and/or Autism). It was a regular day at first, nothing out of the ordinary. But then, around noon, I reached a breaking point. I just had enough of the mess that was in my mind, I was tired of the never-ending feeling of confusion. I needed some clarity and answers.

Since I had been told from a young age that I was "a bit autistic", I decided this was a good place to start. I reached out to AdultAutism.ie, and they asked me to fill out some questionnaires. It was one of these that changed everything. It was the ASRS-v form, the ADHD Self-Report Scale, a tool to help diagnose adult ADHD. I didn't check the results right away, I waited until 4/11/2022 to look at them. I scored very high on ADHD traits, especially inattentive traits. I'm not going to lie, this came as a surprise, I had never considered ADHD as a possibility for me. It had only come up twice in my life, in passing conversation, and never about myself. So, I turned to YouTube and watched some Ted Talks, for some answers.

After just two, I was crying. Two women had spoken about my life, my struggles, and my feelings. They had put words to what I had always wanted to express. They made me feel seen and understood. It was like a puzzle coming together. I realized that I was not just the odd one out, the one who was too much of everything, too talkative, too distracted, too emotional, too excited, too quiet, and too sensitive. Always in a state of chaos, fog, and frustration in my mind, never able to catch a thought like it was slippery jelly in my hands. I finally understood what it was. Who I was. It was a complete shift in perspective. In the most wonderful way. Before this, I just thought I was missing something, always on the edge of society, unable to connect the dots. I believed everyone was the same as me but were handling it better. I would procrastinate when it came to cleaning the house, sending an email, making a phone call, and starting an assignment. I was always angry with myself, why was I incapable of something so simple, just do it. I wondered if I was lazy. I had the desire to complete the task, I was sure of that, it was so hard to make that physical push. I thought I was a diligent worker, but I had little evidence to prove it. I doubted my intelligence, that diligent worker was a lie, it was just occasional strokes of luck, I was just deceiving others and myself into thinking I was competent. As I would then face an inevitable bad brain day or week. I would neglect to send an email; I would overlook something important. Most annoying of all I would frequently lose concentration. And I would resort to my most hated of excuses of "I don't know" or "I forgot". I did try, but I was slow and easily side-tracked and easily puzzled.

Following the TedTalk awakening, I realised how little I knew about ADHD. I started to devour every piece of information I could get my hands on. The more I learned, the more I could relate. So, I decided to take the next step and booked an appointment with my doctor to get a referral. I was terrified of this appointment more than the actual diagnosis. I had heard too many horror stories of people being dismissed or denied by their doctors. I was a mess the days leading to the appointment. I kept swinging between excitement and doubt. Maybe I was right, and this was the answer to my struggles. Or maybe, I was wrong, and I was just lazy, dumb, and making excuses. But then I would watch a video on YouTube, especially Jessica McCabe's "How to ADHD", or check out Cherry ADHDs Instagram page, and I felt reassured.

My doctor informed me that the psychiatrist was not taking new patients, it could be a long wait, but "maybe we would be lucky". I was lucky. The day after my doctor appointment the psychiatrist began taking referrals again, and on the 1st of March, I finally met the psychiatrist who would give me some answers. I have ADHD. The relief. After my ADHD appointment, the psychiatrist told me that I also showed clinical signs of Autism, and he would send me questionnaires after the appointment to complete and "see where we go from there". I answered questions about autism in general, sensory issues, masking, repetitive behaviours, and more. The results concluded that "*7 out of 8 of the scores are (decisively) above the screening threshold for autism*".

As I have only been on this journey for a few months, I do not have all the answers, and I still have so much to learn about myself and this diagnosis. But I am delighted to share my journey of self-exploration with you. This understanding and kindness towards myself have already changed my entire outlook. It gave me the incentive to look back at my life, understanding how, why, and where I struggled, how I handled it, even maybe subconsciously, to mitigate the effects. Many of the methods to "assist" myself were not healthy and I have to unlearn these bad habits and reteach myself how to think and act. I hope going on this journey will help me learn new skills and habits that can support me. So, I hope you view this book as I intend, to honour you, and to reassure you that you are not damaged or imperfect. You are amazing, just the way you are. You do not have to fit in with the social standards or expectations that others may have of you. You have your journey and your mission in this world.

This book is a message of affection and acceptance for yourself and others.

Not so long after my diagnosis, I had a "Eureka moment", I had been stifling my creativity for a very long time. Instead, I was concentrating on merely ticking boxes every day. This realisation was the wake-up call I needed. I had been living a lie, pretending to be someone I was not, doing things I didn't enjoy. I had lost touch with my true self, my creative spirit. I had hidden away all my art supplies, afraid to use them. But now, I felt liberated. I had freed myself from the shackles of self-doubt and conformity. I'm drawing again, writing, and letting my imagination run wild. There is nothing wrong with daydreaming. I just need to stop caring about what others think. I do still struggle, of course, especially while I'm working on this book. I wonder if I have what it takes to write something meaningful and engaging. I have a dream of writing a novel someday, but I often doubt myself and criticise my abilities. How could I think of myself as a writer? But then I remember, even if the novel never gets published, it would be an accomplishment to finish it. My accomplishment and that's what motivates me. Speaking of book writing, the next two chapters will be used to communicate everything I learned these last few months, so I will be going full nerd until chapter 4. I'm not going to lie I love full research mode, I live for it, however, not everyone will enjoy it. If you do not like that you can head straight to chapter 4 and the memoir. No judgement from this end at all.

And a final message to you; You are unique, you may not follow the "social" standards that are in place for what "normal" is, but that's ok. The message of this book is nothing is wrong with you, you are magnificent, and you should not feel lost in this world and yourself.

Chapter 2
ADHD and Autism (A background)

Attention-Deficit/ Hyperactivity Disorder (ADHD) and Autism Spectrum Disorder (ASD) are both neurodevelopmental disorders. In the DSM-5 (Diagnostic and Statistical Manual of Mental Disorders, fifth edition) there are many areas of overlap between them, and while some of these overlaps are acknowledged in the criteria, many are not. For example, executive function issues are common in both conditions. This means people with ADHD and/or Autism may struggle with decision-making, impulse control, time management, focus, organisation skills and emotional regulation. However, these problems are not considered among the diagnostic criteria for Autism. In Autism, social skills, sensory processes, and restrictive-repetitive behaviours are examined. While many with ADHD may also tend to be limited in these ways, they are not generally considered in the official criteria. ADHD is diagnosed based on the presence of attention deficit, hyperactivity, and impulsivity.

For many years doctors did not like to diagnose a person with both ADHD and Autism and were considered mutually exclusive. If a patient presented with symptoms of both conditions, the clinician had to choose which diagnosis fit best. It wasn't until 2013 with the release of the DSM-5 that both were considered to co-occur. This was a significant change from the previous edition, which stated that a diagnosis of Autism ruled out the possibility of ADHD. This change has opened new avenues for research and treatment of this common comorbidity.

Shockingly, in Ireland, if a child is diagnosed with ADHD after a diagnosis of Autism the support, they had been receiving for autism could be dropped. Even when research such as the review by Yael Leitner in 2014 shows that the prevalence of ADHD among people with Autism ranges from 30 to 80%, while Autism traits among people with ADHD range from 20 to 50%. These numbers indicate that there is a substantial overlap between the two disorders and that they may share some underlying genetic or environmental factors. Both Autism and ADHD are characterised by impairments in social communication, attention, executive functioning, and behavioural regulation, but they also have distinct features that differentiate them from each other. Understanding the similarities and differences between these two conditions is crucial in providing an accurate diagnosis and effective intervention.

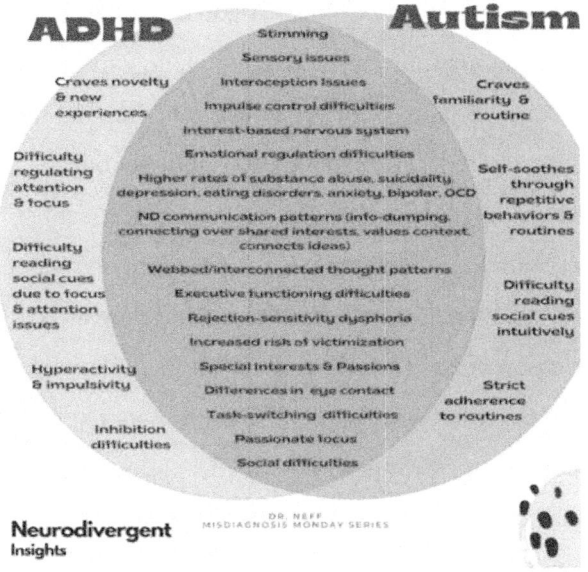

ADHD   **Autism**

Stimming

Sensory issues

Craves novelty   Interoception issues   Craves
& new   familiarity &
experiences   Impulse control difficulties   routine

Interest-based nervous system

Difficulty   Emotional regulation difficulties
regulating   Self-soothes
attention   Higher rates of substance abuse, suicidality,   through
& focus   depression, eating disorders, anxiety, bipolar, OCD   repetitive
                                                            behaviors &
                  ND communication patterns (info-dumping,   routines
              connecting over shared interests, values context,
Difficulty   connects ideas)
reading
social cues   Webbed/interconnected thought patterns
due to focus   Difficulty
& attention   Executive functioning difficulties   reading
issues   social cues
                  Rejection-sensitivity dysphoria   intuitively

                  Increased risk of victimization

Hyperactivity   Special Interests & Passions
& impulsivity   Strict
                  Differences in eye contact   adherence
                                                        to routines
                  Task-switching difficulties
Inhibition
difficulties   Passionate focus

                  Social difficulties

Neurodivergent   DR. NEFF
Insights   MISDIAGNOSIS MONDAY SERIES

According to a study published in 2011 conducted by Vora and Sikora, using data from the Autism Treatment Network (ATN) Registry (a patient registry for children and adolescents with Autism Spectrum Disorder) ADHD and Autism often co-occur and this combination is associated with a lower quality of life and poorer adaptive functioning than having either condition alone. Another study conducted in 2012 led by Sikora found that children with Autism and clinically significant ADHD symptoms had more behavioural problems and lower social skills than children with Autism and fewer ADHD symptoms. The exact causes of both Autism and ADHD are not fully understood, but there seems to be some overlap in the genetic and neurobiological factors that contribute to both conditions. A paper published in 2019 led by Satterstrom reported that genetic variants, especially rare variants, play a major role in the occurrence of both Autism and ADHD and that one particular gene, known as "KDM5A", was significantly associated with both disorders. This gene is involved in regulating the expression of other genes and may affect brain development and function. This could explain why both co-occur. However, this gene alone cannot explain the co-occurrence of Autism and ADHD, and more research is needed to understand how different genes interact with each other and the environment to influence the development of these conditions.

Time to get into Autism and ADHD, and the current state of knowledge.

Autism spectrum disorder is a developmental condition that affects how people communicate and interact with others. Autistic individuals may have different levels of abilities and challenges, and they may experience the world in different ways. There is no single way to be autistic, and each person with Autism is unique. These symptoms vary along a spectrum, hence the **name Autism Spectrum Disorder**. However, three core symptoms are common to all forms of Autism. They are social interaction difficulties: such as reduced eye contact, an apparent lack of empathy, and poor social skills.

Communication challenges: such as delayed speech, echolalia, and trouble with nonverbal cues. And **restricted and repetitive behaviours**: such as spinning, lining up objects, and hand flapping.

One of the main methods to differentiate the severity of Autistic traits among people is to use the levels of support that they may need in their daily life. These levels are based on how much difficulty they have with social communication and restricted or repetitive behaviours. The levels are:

ASD level 1: This is sometimes called high-functioning autism or mild autism. People with ASD level 1 may have some challenges with social skills, such as understanding nonverbal cues or maintaining a conversation. They may also have some repetitive behaviours or narrow interests that interfere with their flexibility or adaptability. However, they can usually speak and learn without much difficulty, and they may not need a lot of support in their daily life.

ASD level 2: This is sometimes called moderate autism. People with ASD level 2 may have more noticeable difficulties with social communication and interaction. They may have trouble initiating or responding to social interactions, and they may speak in simple or odd ways. They may also have more frequent or intense repetitive behaviours or narrow interests that limit their ability to function in different settings. They may need some support or assistance in their daily life.

ASD level 3: This is sometimes called severe autism or low- functioning autism. People with ASD level 3 may have very limited or no verbal communication skills, and they may have severe challenges with social interaction and understanding. They may also have very rigid or repetitive behaviours or narrow interests that cause significant impairment in their daily life. They may need a lot of support or assistance in their daily life.

These levels are not fixed or permanent, and they may change over time depending on the person's development, environment, and interventions. They are also not meant to label or judge the person's abilities or potential, but rather to help identify their needs and strengths.

Aspergers Syndrome is a term usually associated with Autism, while it is still in use, it is no longer used in the current diagnostic manual (DSM-5) published by the American Psychiatric Association in 2013. Instead, people who would have been diagnosed with Asperger's syndrome in the past are now considered to have ASD level 1.

Another term that is no longer present in the DSM-5 is **pervasive developmental disorder-not otherwise specified** (PDD-NOS) or **atypical autism**. While not as well known, it tends to have a more sociological and behavioural deviation and is a less studied type of autism. This term was used to describe people who had some signs of autism but did not meet the full criteria for ASD or Asperger's syndrome. PDD-NOS was also removed from the DSM-5 and replaced by Autism Spectrum Disorder with a severity rating. People who were diagnosed with PDD-NOS before 2013 may benefit from a re-evaluation and updated treatment recommendations.

There is a significant gender disparity in the prevalence of the condition. According to a 2021 study by Concetta de Giambattista and colleagues, ASD affects boys more than girls, with a ratio of 4.2:1. This implies that for every autistic girl, there are four autistic boys. Historically, girls were not thought to be autistic, and this may have influenced the diagnosis and treatment of ASD in different genders. However, some studies suggest that this gap may narrow or even disappear in adulthood, as more females are identified later in life. This gap may be due to girls being more likely to mimic social cues and hide their autistic traits than boys, a phenomenon known as masking. Moreover, society tends to accept certain behaviours that are stereotypically female, such as being introverted, quiet or shy. Therefore, a girl who is silent in class and does not cause trouble may not be noticed as having ASD (this is not always the case, as I experienced selective mutism in primary school and my teacher flagged it as a concern... but nothing much came out of it, due to how little knowledge was available in the 90's).

Researchers suggest that the gender gap in ASD may be due to these missed clinical signs in girls, which suggests that many may remain undiagnosed and untreated. As a result, girls may face more challenges in accessing support services, which can affect their mental health and well-being. Thus, it is vital to recognize that autism can present differently in boys and girls and to develop gender-specific diagnostic tools and interventions.

Autism in Boys	Autism in Girls
Inept at responding to non-verbal cues and gaze following.	• Can respond to non-verbal cues and gaze following
Obsession over unusual interests such as statistics and schedules*	• Obsession over more acceptable interests such as TV shows.
Can display more aggressive behaviour.	• Can be passive
Tend to struggle with social communication from an early age.	• Generally, struggle with communication later in life

Attention-Deficit/ Hyperactivity Disorder is better known for its shortened form of ADHD. Until 1987 ADHD was referred to as ADD- Attention Deficit Disorder and had been described as an executive function disorder. ADHD is based on the symptoms of inattention and hyperactivity or impulsivity. An ADHD diagnosis is based on determinants of these symptoms:

Predominantly inattentive type: People with this type have difficulty paying attention to details, following instructions, organizing tasks, or listening to others. They may make careless mistakes, lose things, or get distracted easily.

Predominantly hyperactive-impulsive type: People with this type have difficulty sitting still, waiting their turn, or keeping quiet. They may fidget, run around, interrupt others, or act without thinking. This type of ADHD is the most recognisable and often diagnosed in boys as children, while it is the most recognisable type, it is the rarest diagnosis of ADHD.

Combined type: People with this type have symptoms of both inattention and hyperactivity-impulsivity. The diagnosis of this type of ADHD requires at least six symptoms of inattention and/or hyperactivity-impulsivity that are inappropriate for the person's developmental level and cause significant impairment in daily functioning.

To diagnose ADHD, a healthcare provider will use the criteria from the Diagnostic and Statistical Manual of Mental Disorders (DSM-5). The provider will ask about the person's symptoms, how long they have been present, how they affect different areas of life (such as home, school, or work), which have persisted for six months, and been present since before the age of 12 and cannot be better explained by a different condition.

The provider will also gather information from parents, teachers, or other adults who know the person well.

ADHD can cause many challenges for people who have

it, such as poor academic or work performance, relationship problems, substance abuse, or low self-confidence. However, ADHD can also have some positive aspects, such as creativity, curiosity, energy, and resilience. With proper treatment and support, we can lead successful and fulfilling lives. More importantly, we will be comfortable with who we are.

Treatment for ADHD may include medication, psychotherapy, behavioural interventions, or a combination of these.

Medication can help reduce the symptoms of ADHD by increasing the levels of neurotransmitters in your brain that regulate attention and activity. Psychotherapy can help people with ADHD cope with their emotions, improve their self-esteem, and learn new skills to manage their behaviour. Behavioural interventions can help people with ADHD change their habits and routines to reduce distractions and increase focus. I go into greater detail on treatments in Chapter 10.

ADHD itself is not specifically an attention deficit, it is trouble allotting this attention where it is required at the time. Trying to focus on something our brain has no interest in is incredibly difficult, almost painful. For me, my vision will blur with the amount of energy I try to put into concentrating, my neck gets tense, and I get a headache on the top of my head. If I am forced to concentrate for a long period, for example, long meetings, it will result in severe migraines lasting at least two days.

Once again, just like in Autism, ADHD is diagnosed and treated more often in males than in females. Research by Erik Skogli and his team in 2013 on gender differences suggests that males are more likely to be diagnosed with ADHD than females, partly because they tend to show more externalising symptoms, such as hyperactivity and impulsivity, that are easier to notice and cause more disruption. Females, on the other hand, often have more internalising symptoms, such as inattention and low self-esteem, that may go unnoticed, or the behaviour is attributed to other factors. Females with ADHD may also face more challenges with depression, anxiety, and coping skills than males with ADHD. The subtype of ADHD that is more prevalent in females is the inattentive presentation, while males are more likely to have the hyperactive presentation. These gender differences may have implications for the treatment and support of people with ADHD.

ADHD in Boys:	**ADHD in Girls:**
• Impulsivity	• Disorganisation
• Fidgeting	• Forgetfulness
• Calling out in class	• Inability to focus or daydreaming.
• Physical outbursts	• Incomplete assignments
• Inattentiveness	• Struggles to keep friends

Living with Autism and ADHD feels like being trapped in a paradox. I have a hard time separating the effects of each condition on my life. I think this shows how complex and messy Autism-ADHD is. My brain needs order and routine, but it also makes me bored and restless, so I crave the thrill of chaos. But when there is no order and routine, I feel more anxious and unsettled. Socialising is another area where this paradox affects me. I have difficulties with social communication, I get overstimulated, and I enjoy being with others but then I feel drained afterwards. Sometimes I am so tired that I can't leave my room or house for days. Routine and being able to have time with my special interests have very strong calming effects. When I can hyperfocus on something I love, I feel happy and calm, helping to keep my mind clear, which is very important for me.

So, I'll now ask this question: Do you consider ADHD or/and Autism a disability? These conditions are classified as developmental disabilities, which means they affect how a person grows and learns. They are not the same as learning disabilities, which affect specific skills like reading or math. People with developmental disabilities have the right to receive accommodations in their work and school environments, such as extra time, breaks, or assistive technology. However, some people may feel reluctant to ask for these accommodations, because they don't want to label themselves as disabled. I think this is the wrong way of thinking. I compare it to my situation of having poor eyesight. Without glasses or contacts, I see very little, just blurry blobs. Does that make me disabled? Maybe, but I don't let it stop me from living my life. I use glasses and contacts to correct my vision and make it easier for me to function and it is never questioned. Asking for help for ADHD and Autism related challenges should be seen in the same way as wearing glasses.

Chapter 3
My Neurodivergent Dictionary

The definitions in this chapter were originally in Chapter 2, however, due to the endless growth of terms I felt they deserved a chapter of their own. I also wanted to give the readers a choice to skip or read them, depending on their interest level.

This chapter will cover all the aspects, features, and challenges of both conditions, some of which may appear in other chapters as well. To make it easier for you to find what you are looking for, I have arranged them in alphabetical order. Here are the topics that you will find in this chapter:

<u>Title</u>
1. ADHD paralysis
2. Alexithymia
3. Anxiety
4. Auditory Processing Disorder
5. Autism Burnout
6. Central coherence
7. Delayed
8. Depressive Disorder
9. Echolalia
10. Echopraxia
11. Emotional Dysregulation
12. Empathy
13. Executive Dysfunction
14. Gastrointestinal issues
15. Gender

Dysphoria
16. Highly Focused or Intense Interests
17. Hyperfocus and/or Hyperfixation
18. Hyperlexia
19. Hypersensitivity & Hyposensitivity
20. Imposter Syndrome Interoception.
21. Masking
22. Mirror Touch Synaesthesia
23. Neurodivergence
24. Object
Permanence
25. Oppositional Defiant Disorder
26. Pathological Demand Avoidance
27. Perfectionist
28. Premenstrual Dysphoric Disorder (PDD)
29. Procrastination
30. Prosopagnosia
31. Rejection
Sensitive Disorder or Rejection Sensitivity
32. Selective mutism
33. Sensory processing Disorder
34. Stimming
35. Theory of Mind
36. Time Blindness

Common Learning difficulties as comorbidities of ADHD and Autism:

1) Development Language Disorder
2) Dyscalculia
3) Dysgraphia
4) Dyslexia
5) Dysphasia
6) Dyspraxia

<u>ADHD Paralysis</u> is a term that describes the difficulty that some people with ADHD have in making decisions or taking action when they are faced with too many options, stimuli, or expectations. It is a state of being stuck and unable to move forward, mentally, or physically. ADHD Paralysis can affect people with ADHD in various situations, such as choosing what to wear, planning a project, or starting a task. It can also cause them to miss deadlines, forget appointments, or neglect responsibilities. Unlike deliberate procrastination, which is an avoidance of something unpleasant or challenging for a short period to gather the real facts. ADHD Paralysis is an involuntary response to feeling overwhelmed or anxious.

People with ADHD often have trouble with "cold decisions", which are not time-sensitive or emotionally charged. They may struggle to weigh the pros and cons, prioritize the options, or commit to a choice. On the other hand, they may excel at "hot decisions", which are immediate and urgent. They may act quickly and confidently in a crisis using their intuition and creativity. For instance, when my son was choking on a piece of food, I instantly grabbed him and performed the Heimlich manoeuvre without hesitating or panicking. My son was then sitting back on my lap before either he or my husband had even registered what had happened.

There are 3 main types of ADHD paralysis:

- **ADHD mental paralysis**: This happens when someone with ADHD is exposed to too much stimulation, such as noise, emotions, or information. Their brain becomes overloaded and shuts down, making it hard to process anything or respond appropriately. You may feel stuck, confused, or blank.

- **ADHD choice paralysis**: This occurs when someone with ADHD must choose from many options or alternatives. They may spend a lot of time analysing the pros and cons of each option, but never reach a conclusion. They may feel overwhelmed, anxious, or indecisive.

- **ADHD task paralysis**: This is when someone with ADHD has trouble starting or completing a task. They may lack motivation, confidence, or focus. They may procrastinate or avoid the task by doing something else or zoning out. They may feel frustrated, guilty, or hopeless.

ADHD paralysis can interfere with daily functioning and cause stress and frustration for people with ADHD and those around them. However, there are ways to overcome it, such as breaking down tasks into smaller steps, setting deadlines and reminders, seeking help or support from others, and using strategies to cope with emotions and distractions.

Alexithymia is a term that means "no words for emotion" in Greek. It is not a mental disorder, but a neuropsychological phenomenon that affects how people experience, identify, and express their emotions. People with alexithymia have trouble understanding their feelings and those of others. They may also have difficulty communicating their emotions verbally or nonverbally. Alexithymia can be associated with some mental health conditions, such as depression, PTSD, and

eating disorders, but also can be present in Autistic

individuals. About 10% of the general population and 20% of autistic people have alexithymia.

One of the challenges of having alexithymia is that it can impair social relationships and emotional well-being.

They may also have trouble coping with stress and regulating their emotions. For example, someone with alexithymia might feel overwhelmed by loud noises or unpleasant smells, but not know why or how to calm themselves down. They might also snap or meltdown without warning because they don't notice the signs of emotional arousal in their body.

However, there are ways to cope with alexithymia and improve emotional awareness and expression. One of them is to seek professional help from a therapist who can teach strategies to identify and label emotions, such as using emotion words, rating scales, or emojis.

Another way is to pay attention to physical sensations, such as muscle tension, heart rate, or breathing patterns, that might indicate an emotional state. A third way is to use essential oils, music, or other sensory stimuli that can help soothe or stimulate emotions. By learning to recognise and communicate their emotions better, people with alexithymia can enhance their quality of life and social interactions. The Neurodivergent Women podcast episode on Interoception & Alexythemia discussed a recent study that examined the impact of emotional literacy on students' behaviour and academic outcomes. Emotional literacy is the ability to recognise, understand, and express one's own emotions and those of others. The study found that when teachers consistently incorporated emotional literacy activities into their lessons, such as naming emotions, identifying triggers, and practising coping skills, there was a significant decline in behavioural issues, detentions, and suspensions among the students. The students also reported feeling more engaged, motivated, and confident in their learning.

Anxiety is an emotional state that involves feeling fearful and alert in response to a perceived danger. It is a natural and adaptive reaction that helps us cope with challenging situations, everyone can have feelings of anxiety at some point in their life. For example, you may feel anxious about an exam or a job interview. During times like these, feeling anxious can be perfectly normal. However, when anxiety becomes excessive and persistent, it can interfere with daily functioning and well-being. Anxiety is often co-occurring with other conditions such as ADHD and Autism, which can affect social and adaptive skills. Sometimes, neurodivergence can be mistaken for anxiety, especially in females and nonbinary individuals. As Sharon Kaye-O'Connor, a licensed clinical social worker in New York City explains, *"Neurodivergence is often misidentified as anxiety, especially in girls, women, and nonbinary folks. Anxiety is often a diagnosis that happens on the way to identifying neurodivergence"*.

Auditory processing disorder (APD), also known as central auditory processing disorder (CAPD) is a condition where the brain has trouble processing and interpreting sounds, especially speech. People with APD have normal hearing, but they often struggle to understand what they hear, especially in noisy environments or when multiple people are talking. APD can affect about 3%–5% of school-aged children, but it can also develop later in life due to factors such as head injury, stroke, or ear infections.

APD is not the same as other conditions that can affect hearing and communication, such as dyslexia, autism spectrum disorder (ASD), or attention deficit hyperactivity disorder (ADHD). However, APD can co-occur with these conditions and cause similar difficulties. For example, many people with ASD or ADHD have trouble making sense of speech in the presence of background noise and other people talking. APD may also affect attention and executive function, which are skills that help us plan, organize, and complete tasks. Stimulant medication may help some people with both APD and ADHD by strengthening the signal from the ear to the brain.

There is no cure for APD, but there are ways to manage it and improve listening and communication skills. Some of the treatments for APD include:

Auditory training: This involves exercises that help train the brain to analyze sounds better and improve speech recognition. Auditory training can be done with a hearing specialist or online.

Compensatory strategies: These are techniques that help people with APD cope with their difficulties and enhance their strengths. For example, using visual aids, repeating, or rephrasing information, asking for clarification, and using memory or problem-solving skills.

Environmental modifications: These are changes that can be made to reduce background noise and improve sound quality. For example, using carpeting and soft furnishings, wearing a wireless earpiece that connects to a microphone worn by a teacher or speaker, or using assistive listening devices.

APD can be challenging, but with proper diagnosis and treatment, people with APD can learn to communicate more effectively and enjoy their daily activities.

Autism Burnout is a term that refers to the state of chronic exhaustion, loss of skills, and reduced tolerance to a stimulus that some autistic individuals experience as a result of chronic life stress and a mismatch of expectations and abilities without adequate support.

According to a 2020 study by Raymaker and colleagues, Autism burnout is a *"syndrome conceptualized as resulting from chronic life stress and a mismatch of expectations and abilities without adequate support. It is characterised by pervasive, long-term (typically 3+months) exhaustion, loss of function, and reduced tolerance to stimulus"*.

Autism burnout is different from depression and work burnout, which have different symptoms and causes. Depression is a mood disorder that affects how a person feels, thinks, and behaves. It can cause persistent feelings of sadness, hopelessness, guilt, and loss of interest in activities. Depression can also affect a person's sleep, appetite, energy, and concentration. Some of the signs of depression that are not typical of autism burnout are anhedonia (reduced ability to feel pleasure), sleep problems, suicidal thoughts or behaviours, and low self-esteem. In contrast, autism burnout does not necessarily involve changes in mood or affect, but rather a loss of function and increased difficulty coping with everyday demands.

While work burnout is a type of occupational stress that occurs when a person feels overwhelmed, emotionally drained, and unable to meet the expectations or demands of their work. Work burnout affects a person's motivation, performance, and satisfaction at work. So, the signs of work burnout revolve around work such as cynicism or detachment from work, feelings of reduced professional ability, and bringing work-related problems home. In contrast, autism burnout is not limited to work-related stressors but can also result from other sources of life stress such as masking, transitions, social pressures, and sensory overload.

While someone with autistic burnout will feel chronically stressed due to social demands, sensory stressors masking, and fatigue associated with the pressures of living and working in a neurotypical world. Autistic burnout can have serious consequences for the well-being and functioning of autistic people. It can affect their health, mental health, independence, self-confidence, and quality of life. Therefore, it is important to recognize the signs of autism burnout and seek help when needed. Some possible ways to prevent or reduce autism burnout are acceptance and support from others, being autistic without hiding or suppressing one's traits or needs, formal accommodations or services that address one's challenges and strengths, self-care, and

coping strategies that reduce stress and promote relaxation. They also need to be able to be themselves and engage in activities that bring them joy and comfort, such as stimming, pursuing their interests, or using comfort items. They may also benefit from formal support, such as therapy, medication, or accommodations at school or work. Autistic burnout is a real and serious phenomenon that deserves more attention.

The study which was led by Dora Raymaker gave some advice on how to deal with Autistic burnout being able to reduce masking, and *"Dealing honestly with scary and difficult emotions might actually be a way to prevent burnout. By allowing people to complain and be heard the difficulties can be overcome and the person is actually more likely to be able to put them aside and work again"*

"Advice I would give. It's okay to—you know, okay to say no if people.... Are asking things of you that you don't feel like you can handle. Listen and respect when your boundaries are being crossed. Asking for help I wish I had known much earlier on that there was no shame in needing or requesting accommodations. If I could redo things, I would likely have tried to acknowledge the contribution of sensory issues to, say, meltdowns at work and put measures in place to better manage them. Learning to be able to ask and accept help from trusted authorities (Ask and Tell by Stephen Shore is a good book). Asking for help and accepting help is an important skill to succeed through autistic burnout.

Breathing exercises, regular exercise, doing activities that bring you joy as a way to decompress. Something as simple as petting an animal, meditation, the ability to exercise in short spurts or do something mindless like watch a funny video or squeeze a stress ball. That'll help ease the oncoming tension and I can float back down to earth gracefully".

Autistic fatigue is a state of extreme mental, physical and/or sensory exhaustion. It can result from overworking the body's resources and can lead to burnout. Autistic fatigue has often been described as exhaustion with additional difficulties such as increased meltdowns and sensory sensitivity, physical pain, and headaches.

If you think you might be experiencing autistic fatigue, it is important to take time off and rest. You can also use energy accounting which is a system used to set manageable limits on your energy levels, so you do not overwork your body's resources. Making time for interests that re-energize you, having time off school or work and 'unmasking' can all help you recover from fatigue and burnout.

Another way is to put simple adaptations in place that can help you cope and manage better and reduce the risk of fatigue and burnout. Examples of this include using earplugs to help with sensory overload.

Central coherence is the ability to integrate information from different sources and contexts into a coherent whole. Central coherence and neurodivergence are related concepts that have implications for understanding the diversity of human cognition and behaviour. Some neurodivergent individuals may have lower levels of central coherence, whichmeans they tend to focus on the details rather than the big picture. This can lead to difficulties in understanding social situations, metaphors, humour, or sarcasm, but also to advantages in tasks that require attention to detail, such as pattern recognition, memory recall, or problem-solving. Other neurodivergent individuals may have higher levels of central coherence, which means they tend to integrate information from different sources and contexts into a coherent whole. This can lead to difficulties in switching between tasks, coping with change, or filtering out irrelevant information, but also to advantages in tasks that require holistic thinking, such as creativity, inference, or perspective taking.

Central coherence and neurodivergence are not fixed or static traits, but rather dynamic and context-dependent processes that can vary across individuals and situations over time. This reflects the diversity and complexity of human cognition and behaviour.

Delayed sleep phase syndrome (DSPS) is a circadian rhythm disorder that affects the timing of sleep and wakefulness. People with DSPS have difficulty falling asleep at a conventional bedtime and waking up at a socially acceptable time. They tend to have a delayed sleep-wake phase, meaning that their biological clock is shifted later than the norm. DSPS can cause significant impairment in daily functioning, such as school, work, and social activities.

DSPS is often associated with neurodivergent conditions, such as ADHD, Autism, bipolar disorder, and depression. The exact relationship between DSPS and these conditions is not fully understood, but some possible explanations are:

Genetic factors: Some genes involved in regulating the circadian rhythm may also influence the development of neurodivergence. For example, mutations in the CLOCK gene have been linked to both DSPS and bipolar disorder.

Environmental factors: Exposure to light, especially blue light from electronic devices, can affect the circadian rhythm and delay the onset of sleep. People with neurodivergence may be more prone to using these devices at night or have difficulty regulating their screen time.

Behavioural factors: People with neurodivergence may have irregular sleep habits, such as staying up late, napping during the day, or having variable bedtimes.

These behaviours can disrupt the circadian rhythm and exacerbate DSPS symptoms.

Psychological factors: People with neurodivergence may experience more stress, anxiety, or mood swings than neurotypical people. These emotions can interfere with sleep quality and quantity, as well as affect the circadian rhythm.

The treatment of DSPS involves adjusting the sleep-wake cycle to align with the desired schedule. This can be achieved by:

Practicing good sleep hygiene: This includes having a regular bedtime and wake-up time, avoiding caffeine, alcohol, and nicotine before bed, limiting exposure to light at night and increasing it in the morning, and creating a comfortable and quiet sleeping environment.

Using chronotherapy: This is a method of gradually shifting the sleep-wake cycle by delaying bedtime and wake-up time by 1-2 hours each day until the desired schedule is reached. For example, if someone normally goes to bed at 2 a.m. and wakes up at 10 a.m., they will go to bed at 3 a.m. and wake up at 11 a.m. on the first day, then 4 a.m. and 12 p.m. on the second day, and so on.

Using bright light therapy: This involves exposing oneself to bright light for a certain duration and intensity at specific times of the day. The light stimulates the production of melatonin, a hormone that regulates the circadian rhythm. For people with DSPS, bright light therapy is usually recommended in the morning to advance the sleep phase.

Using melatonin supplements: Melatonin is a natural hormone that helps regulate the circadian rhythm. Taking melatonin supplements before bedtime can help induce sleepiness and advance the sleep phase. However, melatonin should be used with caution and under medical supervision, as it may have side effects or interact with other medications.

DSPS is a challenging condition that can affect many aspects of life. However, with proper diagnosis, treatment, and support, people with DSPS can improve their sleep quality and quantity, as well as their overall well-being.

Depressive disorder (Also known as depression) is a common mental disorder that affects how a person feels, thinks, and behaves. It is characterised by a persistent feeling of sadness and loss of interest in activities that used to be enjoyable. Depression can interfere with daily functioning and cause various physical and emotional problems. Depression is not a sign of weakness or a character flaw. It is a serious condition that requires professional help.

Depression can be triggered or worsened by various factors, such as stressful life events, trauma, abuse, loss, illness, genetics, hormones, or brain chemistry. Some people may be more vulnerable to depression than others due to their personality, coping skills, or social support. Depression can also co-occur with other mental disorders, such as Autism and ADHD. The challenges those with ADHD and Autism encounter in managing their emotions, attention, impulses, and social skills can lead to low self-esteem, negative self-image, frustration, isolation, and discrimination. All of these factors can increase the risk of developing depression.

According to some studies, people with ADHD are more than twice as likely to have depression than people without ADHD. A survey conducted in 2017 by a team led by Katzman found that about 18.6% of people with ADHD will experience depression in their lifetimes, compared with reported comorbid ADHD in individuals with depression is at a rate of 7.8%. Similarly, research suggests that autistic people may be more likely to experience depression than non-autistic people. A 2019 meta-analysis led by Chloe Hudson showed that autistic people are four times more likely to experience depression than those who are not autistic. The study estimated that 40% of autistic adults and 8% of autistic children and adolescents have had depression.

Depression is treatable and with the right support, you can feel better. The first step is to seek help from a qualified mental health professional who can diagnose your condition and offer you appropriate treatment options. Treatment for depression may include psychotherapy (also known as talk therapy), medication, or a combination of both. Psychotherapy can help you understand your feelings, thoughts, and behaviours and learn coping skills to deal with stress and challenges.

Medication can help balance the chemicals in your brain that affect your mood and emotions. Sometimes, other interventions such as exercise, relaxation techniques, or light therapy may also be helpful.

One of the challenges in diagnosing and treating depression in people with autism or ADHD is the overlap in symptoms. Some of the symptoms of depression, such as low mood, reduced appetite, sleep problems, low energy, social withdrawal, and reduced communication can also be part of the autism or ADHD spectrum. Therefore, it is important to consider the person's developmental history and baseline functioning when assessing their mental health status. A 2020 study led by Farhad Montazeri found that depression in autistic children often shows up as insomnia and restlessness rather than feelings of sadness. Thus, it is essential to look for subtle signs of depression and ask the person how they feel rather than relying on their outward appearance.

If you think you or someone you know may have depression, do not hesitate to reach out for help. Depression is not something you have to deal with alone. There are many resources and support groups available for people with depression and co-occurring conditions such as autism or ADHD. You can also talk to your family doctor, school counsellor, teacher, friend, or family member who can guide you to the right services. Remember that depression is common and treatable, and you deserve to feel better.

Echolalia is the repetition of words or phrases that are spoken by another person. It is a common feature of some developmental and neurological disorders, such as autism spectrum disorder, Tourette syndrome, and schizophrenia. Echolalia can be immediate or delayed and can be voluntary or involuntary. Echolalia can serve different functions depending on the context and the individual. Some possible functions are communication, self-regulation, rehearsal, scripting, and social interaction. Echolalia can also indicate a lack of comprehension or a need for support. Echolalia is not a disorder by itself, but rather a symptom of an underlying condition. Therefore, it is important to assess the function and meaning of echolalia for each person and to provide appropriate interventions and strategies to enhance their communication and social skills.

Echopraxia is a term that refers to the involuntary copying of another person's movements or actions. It is a type of echo-phenomenon, which is a general term for automatic imitative behaviours that occur without conscious awareness or intention. Echopraxia can be seen in various mental and neurological conditions, such as schizophrenia, Tourette syndrome, Autism, catatonia, epilepsy, dementia, and some culture-bound syndromes. The exact cause of echopraxia is not fully understood, but some researchers suggest that it may involve abnormalities in the mirror neuron system, which is a network of brain cells that are activated when observing or performing actions. Echopraxia can cause difficulties in social interactions and relationships, as it may be perceived as mocking or inappropriate by others.

Emotional Dysregulation is a common challenge for people with ADHD and Autism. It means having difficulty managing your emotions in a way that matches the situation. For example, you might feel very angry or sad over something small or have trouble calming down after getting upset. You might also act impulsively or have sudden outbursts of emotion. Emotional dysregulation can affect your relationships, your work, your school, and your daily life.

Emotional regulation is the skill of being able to recognize your emotions, identify what they are, and take appropriate actions to keep them from getting out of control. It does not mean hiding or suppressing your emotions, but rather having enough control to make good decisions about how to handle them. For instance, emotional regulation can help you cope with stress, deal with frustration, healthily express your feelings, and bounce back from negative emotions.

People with ADHD and autism may struggle with emotional regulation for different reasons. ADHD can make it hard to focus on your emotions, plan, resist impulses, and switch between tasks. Autism can make it hard to understand your own emotions, read social cues, communicate effectively, and adjust to changes. Both conditions can also make you more sensitive to sensory input, which can trigger strong emotional reactions.

When someone struggles with emotional regulation, they may exhibit some of the following signs:

-Their emotional reactions may seem too intense or too mild for the situation they are in.

-They may be unable to immediately process their

emotions and instead feel them later when the situation is no longer relevant.

-They may have trouble acknowledging or recognizing their own emotions and may try to avoid or suppress them.

-They may not know what they are feeling or why they are feeling it and may have difficulty naming or expressing their emotions.

-They may have trouble moving on from their emotions and may dwell on them for a long time after the situation is over.

-They may find it hard to calm down or soothe themselves after experiencing strong emotions and may feel overwhelmed or out of control.

There are ways to improve your emotional regulation skills if you have ADHD or autism. Some strategies include:

Practicing mindfulness: This means paying attention to the present moment without judging yourself or your emotions. Mindfulness can help you become more aware of your emotions and how they affect your body and mind. You can practice mindfulness by meditating, breathing deeply, doing yoga, or engaging in a relaxing activity.

Seeking professional help: A therapist or counsellor can help you understand your emotions better and teach you coping skills. They can also help you address any underlying issues that may contribute to your emotional dysregulation, such as anxiety, depression, trauma, or low self-esteem.

Taking care of yourself: Your physical health can affect your emotional health. Make sure you get enough sleep, eat well, exercise regularly, and avoid drugs and alcohol. These habits can help you reduce stress and improve your mood.

Finding support: Having people who care about you and understand you can make a big difference in your emotional well-being. You can find support from your family, friends, teachers, mentors, or peers who share your experiences. You can also join a support group or an online community for people with ADHD or autism.

I had never heard of Emotional dysregulation before my diagnosis of ADHD, but it helped explain why my emotions were so intense. I now understood why I feel things so strongly. I love that I am easily excited, but others often ask me to chill out. The worst part is how my anger can flare up and then vanish in a flash. I can also cry over something minor. Emotional dysregulation is a common feature of ADHD, but it's not part of the diagnosis process. That's strange because it affects so many of us with ADHD. The reason? Emotions are hard to quantify, researchers wanted to use criteria they can clearly define and measure, so they dropped it in the 70s. Experts acknowledge that ADHD and Emotional Dysregulation are related, but it's unclear if or when they will change the criteria. It may be added to the criteria in the future, but it may not.

Empathy helps us connect with others and show them our care and support. It means that we can feel what they feel and see things from their perspective. Empathy is essential for building strong and healthy relationships and for making the world a better place.

There are three kinds of empathy that we can practice: Cognitive empathy, Affective empathy (also known as Emotional empathy) and Compassionate empathy. They are different, but they all work together to help us understand and help others.

Cognitive empathy is when we can think like someone else and know what they are going through. We can imagine ourselves in their situation and understand their thoughts and feelings. This kind of empathy helps us communicate better and relate to others more easily.

Emotional empathy is when we can feel what someone else is feeling. We can sense their emotions and share their joy or sorrow, which may lead to someone feeling concerned for another person's well-being, or it may lead to feelings of personal distress. This form of empathy helps us empathise with others and show them our genuine concern.

Compassionate empathy is when we can act on empathy and do something to help someone else. We can feel their pain or happiness and have a desire to make things better for them. This kind of empathy helps us be kind and compassionate to others and make a positive difference in their lives. It is the ability to understand and share in someone else's emotions, without taking them on as your own or blurring the line between you and another person.

People with autism may have difficulties with cognitive empathy, which can affect their social interactions and communication. However, this does not mean that they lack emotions or compassion. Many people with autism have a high level of affective empathy, which is the emotional reaction to the feelings of others. Affective empathy is often instinctive and automatic, and it can be very intense and overwhelming for some people with autism. They may feel the pain, joy, sadness, or anger of others as if it were their own. This can make them very empathetic and caring, but also vulnerable to stress.

Some recent studies suggest that people with autism have a hyperactive mirror neuron system, a brain mechanism that allows us to feel what others feel. Potentially explaining why some people with autism experience affective empathy more strongly than others.

As part of my diagnosis of Autism Spectrum Disorder I was given a questionnaire for Emotional Quotient (EQ), this measures Cognitive empathy and affective empathy, I received a score of 32, which means I have a lower-than-average level of cognitive empathy. However, I also did the Toronto Empathy Questionnaire (TEQ), which measures a person's emotional ability to understand and respond to others, I received a score of 61, which indicates a higher-than-normal emotional empathy.

Executive Dysfunction is a common challenge for people with autism and/or ADHD. It affects how we plan, organise, remember, and act on our goals.

According to Verywell Mind, executive dysfunction is not a diagnosis, but a symptom of ADHD or other conditions that involve differences in the brain regions responsible for executive functions. Executive functions are the mental skills that help us carry out tasks, such as following instructions, managing time, controlling impulses, and switch between tasks. They are essential for success in school, work, and life.

One of the executive functions that people with autism and ADHD may struggle with is working memory. Working memory is the ability to hold and manipulate information in our minds for a short period. For example, we use working memory when we do mental math or remember a phone number. People with autism and ADHD may struggle with working memory because their brains process information differently than neurotypical people. This can make it hard for them to keep track of details, follow directions, or solve problems.

Autistic individuals and ADHDers may have trouble with response inhibition. Response inhibition is a core executive function, it is the ability to think before we act and resist distractions or temptations. For example, we use response inhibition when we wait to speak or avoid checking our phones while driving. People with autism and ADHD may find it hard to control their impulses or filter their thoughts because their brains have less activity in the prefrontal cortex, which is the part of the brain that regulates executive functions. This can lead to impulsive behaviour, blurting our answers, or difficulty focusing.

Executive dysfunction does not mean that people with autism and ADHD are incapable of achieving their goals. There are many strategies and supports that can help them overcome their executive challenges and improve their executive skills. Some examples are using reminders, calendars, timers, checklists, planners, apps, or other tools to organize their tasks and time; breaking down big projects into smaller steps; asking for help or clarification when needed; practising mindfulness or relaxation techniques to cope with stress or emotions; rewarding themselves for completing tasks or reaching milestones; and finding ways to make their work more enjoyable or meaningful.

By using these strategies and supports, people with autism and ADHD can boost their executive functioning and accomplish their goals.

Executive dysfunction is not a flaw or a weakness. It is a difference in how the brain works that can create challenges but also strengths. People with autism and ADHD have many talents and abilities that can help them succeed in life. They are creative, curious, passionate, resilient, and unique. They have highly focused or intense interests and a tendency to focus in-depth on the topics they love.

Highly Focused or Intense Interests, also called Monotropism is a cognitive strategy that is often seen as the core feature of autism. It means that the mind tends to focus on a few interests at a time and ignores or misses other things that are not related to those interests. Monotropism can explain why autistic people highly focused or intense interests and a tendency have to focus in depth to the exclusion of other inputs. These interests can be anything, such as art, music, gardening, animals, postcodes, or numbers. They can start at a young age and change over time or last a lifetime. For some autistic children, their interests can be characters from tv shows, dinosaurs or animals.

Having these intense interests can have many benefits for autistic people. They can help them to relax, feel happy, cope with uncertainty, and find meaning and purpose in their lives. They can also lead to educational and career advantages, as well as social and emotional skills. For example, Rebecca Wood published a paper in 2019, looking at how these special interests in autistic children should be taken into consideration in schools. She argues that supporting these interests can reduce the need for prompting and repetition and increase the empathy and understanding of school staff. She also suggests that these interests can enhance children's learning, creativity, motivation, and self-esteem.

However, there can also be some challenges or drawbacks associated with monotropism. Sometimes, autistic people may have difficulty switching their attention from one interest to another or balancing their interests with other demands or expectations. They may also face stigma or discrimination from others who do not share or appreciate their interests, or who view them as obsessive or abnormal. Therefore, autistic people and their allies need to find ways to respect and celebrate their interests, while also being flexible and adaptable when needed.

Gastrointestinal Issues (GI) are some of the most common medical conditions comorbid with Autism Spectrum (Leader & Mannion, 2016b; Tye et al., 2019). According to a recent study, 82.4% of children and adolescents with ASD experience at least one GI symptom (Leader et al., 2020). The most prevalent GI symptoms in individuals with Autism are abdominal pain, diarrhoea, acid reflux, bloating, nausea, and constipation (Mannion & Leader, 2016; Mannion & Leader, 2013). Children with Autism have an almost eight times higher risk of having one or more chronic GI symptoms compared to children without Autism (Chaidez et al., 2014). Recognizing GI symptoms in people with ASD can be especially challenging, as some individuals are non-verbal and many have impaired communication, making it harder for them to express pain or discomfort (Buie et al., 2010). GI symptoms can also worsen ASD symptoms, such as behavioural problems and social difficulties, and lower the quality of life of individuals with ASD and their families (Madra et al., 2020). Therefore, clinicians need to understand how these GI issues present and apply effective therapies.

Treating GI problems in ASD may result in significant improvements in ASD behavioural outcomes.

Gender dysphoria and autism have been shown to have a potential link according to some studies, but the nature and extent of this connection are still unclear. Gender dysphoria is the feeling of distress or discomfort when one's assigned sex at birth does not match one's gender identity.

Some possible explanations for the association between gender dysphoria and autism are:

Gender dysphoria could be a manifestation of autism, and autistic-like traits could drive gender dysphoria. For instance, a child with a male-assigned gender and autism may become preoccupied with female clothes, toys, and activities. This apparent gender dysphoria may not be gender dysphoria at all but rather OCD.

People who feel significant distress because their gender identity differs from their birth sex have higher- than-expected rates of autism, and people with autism appear to have higher rates of gender dysphoria than the general population. This could suggest a common genetic or hormonal factor that influences both conditions, such as variations in exposure to androgens (male hormones) during prenatal development.

People with autism may have a different perception of gender than non-autistic people and may not conform to social and traditional expectations of gender roles and expression. This could make them more likely to identify as transgender or non-binary, or to experience gender dysphoria if they feel pressured to fit in with their assigned sex.

More research is needed to understand the relationship between gender dysphoria and autism and to develop appropriate assessment tools, support, and treatment for people who experience both conditions. It is important to respect and affirm the gender identity of each individual, regardless of their autism diagnosis, and to provide them with the resources and care they need to live authentically and happily without trying to change them, it is about accepting their true selves not moulding them into what is deemed "normal".

Hyperfocus or/and Hyperfixation are two terms that are often used interchangeably in the literature, but they have different meanings and implications for people with neurodivergent conditions. Hyperfocus is a state of intense concentration on a task or activity that can be beneficial or detrimental depending on the context.

Hyperfixation is a persistent and obsessive interest in a topic or subject that can interfere with other aspects of life. Here are some differences between hyperfocus and hyperfixation:

Hyperfocus is usually triggered by external factors, such as deadlines, rewards, or challenges, while hyperfixation is driven by internal motivation and curiosity.

Hyperfocus can be switched on and off depending on the situation, with hyperfixation breaking away is extremely difficult, even when it causes problems.

Hyperfocus can enhance productivity and creativity, while hyperfixation can impair functioning and social skills.

Hyperfocus is more common in people with ADHD, while hyperfixation is more common in people with autism.

However, these terms are not mutually exclusive, and some people may experience both hyperfocus and hyperfixation at different times or different topics. It is important to recognize the signs and effects of both states and find ways to manage them effectively. Some strategies include:

Setting timers and alarms to remind yourself of other tasks and obligations.

Creating a schedule or a list of priorities to balance your time and energy.

Seeking feedback and support from others who understand your condition and interests.

Finding outlets and hobbies that allow you to express your passion and enthusiasm without compromising your well-being.

Hyperlexia is a term that describes the ability to read

words or sentences beyond the expected level for one's age or developmental stage, often accompanied by difficulties in understanding spoken language, social interactions, and nonverbal cues. Hyperlexia is not a diagnosis, but rather a symptom that may be associated with various conditions, such as Autism, developmental language disorder, or specific language impairment.

Hyperlexia can be classified into three types: hyperlexia I, which is a precocious reading ability in neurotypical children; hyperlexia II, which is a splinter skill in children with autism spectrum disorder; and hyperlexia III, which is an acquired reading ability in children who have experienced a brain injury or environmental deprivation. The causes of hyperlexia are not fully understood, but some possible factors include genetic influences, brain structure and function, and environmental exposure to written language. Hyperlexia can have both advantages and disadvantages for the affected individuals, depending on the type and severity of their condition, as well as the availability of appropriate interventions and support.

Hypersensitivity and Hyposensitivity are common features in those with Autism but are also reported in those with ADHD, with research showing that hypo- and hypersensitivity may be viewed as key features of adult ADHD, and women are more affected than men, with 43% of the females with ADHD reported sensory hyper- and/or hyposensitivity, compared to 22% of the men with ADHD. Hypersensitivity is usually what is considered in those with ADHD this is due to the ADHD brain flooding your system with details. When someone is hypersensitive, their ADHD brain lets in too much information from their surroundings, such as noises, smells, or movements, everything within eyesight rushes into the brain because of the inability to filter out all the extras. This can be overwhelming and result in feelings of stress and anxiety. Research by Lane and Reynolds showed this in a 2019 paper, demonstrating that this triggers the "fight or flight" mode in the nervous system, which can cause emotional outbursts and frustration, while others may not seem bothered at all.

Hyposensitivity is a condition where a person has a reduced or absent response to sensory stimuli. This means that a person with hyposensitivity may not feel sensations such as heat, cold, or pain as intensely as others. They may also have trouble sensing their bodily states, such as hunger or illness. This can lead them to seek more sensory input from their environment, such as touching different textures or moving around a lot.

Hyposensitivity can affect different senses, such as touch, smell, taste, hearing, or vision. I will go further in this when I discuss interoception later in this chapter, which is the ability to sense the internal state of the body.

Imposter syndrome is a common phenomenon among Autistic people and ADHDers. It refers to the feeling of being a fraud or a failure, despite having evidence of success and competence. Many people with ADHD experience imposter syndrome because they must conceal their challenges and difficulties from others.

They may feel like they must work harder than their peers to achieve the same results, and they may worry about being exposed or rejected if their struggles are revealed. Imposter syndrome can also affect their career choices and goals, as they may avoid taking on new opportunities or challenges due to fear of failure or criticism. Hiding part of themselves can also create feelings of shame and guilt and lower their self-esteem.

I cannot believe I almost forgot to add imposter syndrome here as it is undeniably common and is very true to myself. Even while writing this book, that invasive voice in my head would say: "You are not qualified for this, you are just fooling yourself". This is the imposter syndrome talking. I hope while you read this section you can remind yourself you are capable. More than capable.

Imposter syndrome can manifest in different ways, such as:

Dismissing your success as a result of luck, timing, or external factors, rather than your skills, effort, or creativity. You may feel like you don't deserve the praise or recognition you receive for your work, and that you are not as competent as others think you are.

Dwelling on your mistakes and failures, rather than your accomplishments and strengths. You may focus on what you did wrong, rather than what you did right. You may also compare yourself unfavourably to others, believing they have achieved more with less effort or difficulty than you.

Avoid celebrating your success or taking pride in your work. You may feel like you must move on to the next task or challenge immediately, without taking time to enjoy or appreciate what you have done. You may also feel anxious or doubtful about your ability to meet future expectations or goals.

Tick, tick, tick, I said yes to all of these, and even though I am aware of thus, I still doubt myself regularly. To help reduce these feelings, I keep track of what I do, I like writing things down, and now I am trying to step back and look at some of my achievements, hopefully this can help me to fully appreciate the success I have and stop attributing it to luck... Most of the time.

If you identify with any of these signs, you may be experiencing impostor syndrome. However, there are ways to overcome it and boost your confidence and self-esteem. Some of the strategies that can help are:

Keeping a record of your achievements and positive feedback. You can write down what you have accomplished, what skills or qualities you have demonstrated, and what compliments or appreciation you have received from others. This can help you acknowledge and internalize your success and counteract any negative thoughts or beliefs you may have about yourself.

Seeking professional help if needed. If impostor syndrome is affecting your mental health or well-being, you may benefit from cognitive behavioural therapy (CBT) or coaching. These interventions can help you identify and challenge any distorted or irrational thoughts you may have about yourself and your work and replace them with more realistic and positive ones.

Practicing self-compassion and gratitude. You can treat yourself with kindness and respect, rather than harshness and criticism. You can also express gratitude for what you have and what you have done, rather than focusing on what you lack or what you have not done. These practices can help you cultivate a more positive and balanced attitude towards yourself and your work. Interoception is a lesser-known sense that helps you understand and feel what's going on inside your body. It is an internal sensory system in which the physical and emotional states of the person are consciously or unconsciously noticed, recognised, and acted upon.

Interoception includes all the signals from your internal organs, such as your heart, lungs, stomach, bladder, and kidneys. These signals are continuously communicated between the brain and the body, and they can shape your emotions, feelings, and intuition.

Interoception skills are required for a range of basic and more advanced functions, such as knowing when to go to the toilet, hunger recognition or even pain. For example, a person notices their stomach is rumbling and they have a pulling sensation in their abdomen. They recognise this as signalling hunger. They respond by eating something. This sense is important for survival, as it allows you to respond to your body's needs and maintain your physical and mental health, as it can affect a person's ability to self-regulate their emotions and self-manage their biological needs.

Interoception can be improved with practice and training. As interoception occurs in 3 steps:

Perceiving the sensation,

Notice a change in state,

where it is

what is going on, and

Actioning that.

Various exercises can help you utilise these steps and tune in to your body and increase your interoceptive awareness. For example, you can try to feel your heartbeat without touching your chest or practice mindful breathing and notice how it affects your body sensations. By improving your interoception, you may also enhance your emotional regulation, empathy, and well-being.

Personal story: I wet the bed past the age of five. I did not think much of this until I got older, I would love to watch crime shows like criminal minds, cold case, CSI, Without a Trace etc... These shows always referred to bedwetting as something negative, so I wanted to find answers. I searched online and found the same scary explanations, like trauma or psychopathy. The MacDonald Triad came up a lot, this refers to animal cruelty, fire setting and bedwetting in childhood as indicators of later aggressive and violent behaviour. So of course, I questioned whether I was a psychopath. But then I remembered the advice my mum gave me that stopped the bedwetting, to use the toilet before bed, even if I didn't feel like it. Problem Solved. What helped there was no judgement, I was never made to feel bad, but I do remember the shame I imposed on myself. I just missed the signal, and reading my book or daydreaming was just more exciting.

Additionally, low pain sensitivity is another example of interoceptive issues. I have a very low sensitivity to pain, which caused them some serious health emergencies. I didn't feel much pain when my appendix burst or when I had an ectopic pregnancy. I was extremely lucky that other people noticed something was wrong and took me to the hospital. I am now more cautious, recently I had mild stomach discomfort lasting a few days, so to the doctor, I want as I did not want another emergency surgery. It was a stomach ulcer.

Masking (also called camouflaging) is a term I will bring up a bit throughout this book, it is something most people will do, but people with ADHD and Autism do it at a colossal level to the detriment of their mental health. Masking may prevent people from getting diagnosed sooner, which is particularly true in women and girls.

That is why during a diagnosis of autism you will fill out a questionnaire called "The Camouflaging Autistic Traits Questionnaire" (CAT-Q) this is described by EmbraceAutism.com as "*a self-report measure of social camouflaging behaviours in adults. It may be used to identify autistic individuals who do not currently meet diagnostic criteria due to their ability to mask their autistic proclivities.*" It is in short, as it sounds, behaviours that hide or mask aspects of oneself from others, or to 'pass' everyday social interactions. It is a coping strategy, but shouldn't be overly utilised as a 2019 study, by a Eilidh Cage and Zoe Troxell-Whitman found that stress and anxiety were higher in people who routinely masked autistic traits, compared to those who tended to mask less often.

When I mask, I'm inclined to change my tone of voice and talking speed, facial expressions, eye contact, and body language. I am very conscious of what I say, I consider every word coming out of my mouth, who I am talking to, and what they would like me to say (I'm not very good at that). I am hyperaware of my activity level,

I am naturally bouncy and excitable, and everything is exciting, but I'm 33, I'm not supposed to be that excitable. So, they say. I'm changing that, if you do see me around I will very likely be clapping my hands and bouncing.

Masking can start early in childhood as a response to social trauma or pressure, and it can become an unconscious habit over time. Which in no way means we are used to it and fine, quite the opposite. Masking can have negative consequences for the mental and physical health of autistic people. It can cause anxiety, depression, suicidal thoughts, exhaustion, burnout, and identity loss. Masking can be so physically and emotionally exhausting some days I can hardly lift my head. It could mean I have to stay in bed to recuperate and take painkillers for the resulting migraines. Masking can be seen as a way of coping with a world that does not accept or understand neurodiversity, but it can also prevent autistic people from being their authentic selves and finding genuine connections with others.

Mirror-touch synaesthesia is a rare condition that causes a person to feel a similar sensation in the same part or opposite part of the body (such as touch) that another person feels. For example, if someone with this condition were to observe someone touching their cheek, they would feel the same sensation on their cheek. I once believed my relationship with mirror-touch synaesthesia was purely emotions. I pick up the positive and negative emotions in others. his results in me being extremely anxious, stressed and confused during a lot of my childhood. Not understanding what I'm feeling and why, and not being able to explain how I am feeling. This would result in intense migraines which can last days. But on the positive side, if someone is happy, I see an eruption of colour, and I feel extreme excitement and joy. I now realise I also had touch-based, especially when someone was in pain, which drove my sister mad as she thought I was copying her. It was not intentional. I did feel the discomfort.

Some researchers note that mirror-touch synaesthesia is common in individuals with autism. This has been confirmed by a study in 2016, led by the cousin of Sacha Baron-Cohen, Simon Baron-Cohen, however, he suggested that mirror-touch synaesthesia does not relate to increased empathy and is instead associated with some form of autism spectrum disorder. I do not agree with Baron-Cohens theory that autistic people are not empathetic. We may not process the same way, or articulate this, but I wholeheartedly believe we are capable of powerful empathy. Especially towards innocent people and animals. A 2015 study proposes that mirror-touch synaesthesia may stem from bodily awareness and a person's inability to distinguish themself and their experiences from others.

According to an article in the journal Frontiers in Human Neuroscience, researchers have identified two main subtypes of touch synaesthesia. The first type causes a person to feel sensations on the part of their body that mirrors the observed touch. The second type causes a person to feel sensations on the opposite part of their body from the observed touch. Mirror-touch synaesthetes have higher levels of affective and pain empathy than those without the condition, though cognitive empathy differs from person to person. Their emotional experience of the observed touch may differ from the emotional experience of the person being touched (a pleasant touch may be perceived as unpleasant or vice versa).

Neurodivergence and neurodiversity are two related terms that describe the variation of human brains and how they work. Neurodivergence is a noun that refers to the state or condition of having a brain that functions differently from what is considered typical.

Neurodiversity is a noun that refers to the concept or idea that these differences are natural and valuable, and not problems or disorders. The term neurodiversity was coined by Judy Singer, an autistic sociologist, in 1998, originally to refer to autistic people. However, it has since expanded to include other conditions that affect how people think, learn, and behave, such as ADHD, dyslexia, dyspraxia, Tourette syndrome and more.

Neurodivergent people may have different ways of communicating, processing information, expressing emotions, socializing, and coping with stress. They may also have different interests, skills, talents, and perspectives that can enrich society and culture.

Neurodivergence and neurodiversity are not something to be cured or fixed, but rather something to be understood and accepted. Neurodiversity is not a fixed category, but a dynamic and evolving one that reflects the latest research and knowledge in psychology and neuroscience.

Object permanence and ADHD were a topic I had not intended to add, but I've seen this a lot on TikTok and Instagram, so I had to bring it up. ADHDers Do Not have a problem with object permanence. "Out of sight out of mind", Yes. "Out of sight, out of mind'" means that you soon forget about people or things that aren't present at that time, but that is not the same as object permanence. Object permanence is a developmental milestone, it is the understanding that whether an object can be sensed does not affect whether it continues to exist. For example, if you place a toy under a blanket, the child who has achieved object permanence knows it is there and can actively seek it. Object permanence usually develops when the baby is around 8 months old.

A better fit would be the term object constancy. Object constancy *"is the ability to maintain a positive emotional bond with something even when distance and conflicts intrude."* These cognitive challenges can make it hard for people with ADHD to remember things that are not in their immediate attention. For example, we may forget to take our medication if it is hidden in a drawer, or we may forget to reply to a text message or call if we get distracted by something else (Guilty). We may also have trouble keeping track of deadlines, appointments, and bills. This does not mean that people with ADHD don't care about their responsibilities or their relationships. It just means that they need more reminders and support to stay on top of things. As John Kruse, MD, PhD, a San Francisco-based psychiatrist says, "out of sight, out of mind" is a more apt phrase for people with ADHD than "object permanence".

How can people with ADHD cope with object constancy issues?

Some strategies can help people with ADHD improve their object constancy and reduce the negative impacts of their forgetfulness. Here are some examples:

Use visual cues and reminders. Place important items or notes in visible places where you will see them often. For example, put your medication on your nightstand or your keys on a hook by the door. You can also use calendars, alarms, timers, apps, or sticky notes to remind you of what you need to do.

Use auditory cues and reminders. You can also use sounds or voices to jog your memory. For example, you can record yourself saying what you need to do and play it back later. You can also ask someone else to call you or send you a voice message to remind you of something.

Use tactile cues and reminders. You can also use touch or movement to help you remember things. For example, you can wear a bracelet or a ring that reminds you of someone or something. You can also use gestures or actions to help you recall information. For example, you can point to your head to remember your homework or tap your pocket to remember your phone.

Use routines and habits. Having a consistent schedule and structure can help you automate some of your tasks and reduce the need for working memory. For example, you can have a morning routine that includes taking your medication, packing your backpack, and checking your calendar. You can also have a bedtime routine that includes charging your phone, setting your alarm, and reviewing your plans for the next day.

Use external support and accountability. Sometimes, you may need help from others to stay on track and remember things. For example, you can ask a friend or a family member to check in with you regularly or to join you in doing something. You can also use apps, websites, or services that can send you reminders, notifications, or rewards for completing tasks.

Use positive reinforcement and self-compassion. Finally, it is important to acknowledge your efforts and achievements and to be kind to yourself when you make mistakes. For example, you can reward yourself for completing a task or reaching a goal. You can also forgive yourself for forgetting something or missing a deadline. Remember that you are not alone and that many people with ADHD struggle with similar issues.

In Conclusion, Object permanence and ADHD are not directly related, but people with ADHD may have issues with object constancy, which is the ability to remember things without sensory cues. This can affect their daily functioning and their relationships. However, there are ways to cope with these challenges and improve their object constancy skills. By using cues, reminders, routines, support, and positive reinforcement, people with ADHD can overcome their forgetfulness and stay connected with their responsibilities and loved ones.

Oppositional Defiant Disorder (ODD) is a behavioural disorder that affects children and adolescents. It is characterised by a persistent pattern of anger, irritability, defiance, and hostility towards authority figures, such as parents, teachers, and peers. Children with ODD often have difficulty following rules, accepting responsibility, and getting along with others. They may also act in a spiteful and vindictive way, such as saying hurtful things or seeking revenge.

There are different theories about what causes ODD, but no single factor can explain it. Some possible factors include:

Developmental factors: Some researchers suggest that ODD may result from problems in the early stages of development when children learn to separate from their caregivers and become more independent. Children with ODD may have had difficulties in forming secure attachments or coping with frustration and negative emotions.

Learning factors: Some researchers propose that ODD may be influenced by the parenting styles and discipline methods used by caregivers. Children with ODD may have learned to use negative and oppositional behaviours to get attention, avoid unpleasant tasks, or escape from consequences. They may also have been exposed to harsh, inconsistent, or abusive parenting practices that undermined their trust and respect for authority figures.

Biological factors: Some researchers point out that ODD may have a genetic component or be related to certain brain structures or functions. Children with ODD may have inherited a tendency to be more impulsive, emotional, or reactive than others. They may also have abnormalities in the parts of the brain that regulate mood, impulse control, and social behaviour.

ODD is more common in boys than girls before puberty, but the rates become more equal after puberty. ODD often co-occurs with other mental health conditions, such as attention-deficit/hyperactivity disorder (ADHD), conduct disorder, mood disorders, and anxiety disorders. These conditions may worsen the symptoms and outcomes of ODD.

The diagnosis of ODD is based on the presence of certain emotional and behavioural symptoms that last for at least six months and cause significant impairment in various domains of life. The symptoms of ODD include:

Frequent temper tantrums or angry outbursts

Frequent arguments with adults or people in authority

Frequent refusal to comply with requests or rules.

Frequent attempts to annoy or provoke others.

Frequent blaming of others for one's own mistakes or misbehaviours

Frequent expression of resentment or spitefulness.

Frequent use of mean or hateful language when upset.

The severity of ODD can vary depending on how many settings the symptoms occur in (such as home, school, or social situations) and how many relationships are affected by the symptoms (such as family members, friends, or teachers).

ODD is a serious condition that can have negative effects on the child's academic performance, social relationships, self-esteem, and mental health. However, with early intervention and appropriate treatment, children with ODD can learn to manage their emotions, cope with frustration, and constructively express their needs. This can help them improve their behaviour, reduce conflict, and enhance their well-being.

The treatment of ODD involves a combination of psychological and behavioural interventions that aim to improve the child's social skills, emotional regulation, problem-solving abilities, and coping strategies. The treatment also involves working with the parents and other caregivers to provide consistent, positive, and effective parenting practices that support the child's development and reduce conflict. In some cases, medication may be prescribed to treat co-occurring conditions or to reduce severe symptoms of ODD.

Pathological Demand Avoidance (PDA) is a term that describes a pattern of behaviour in which people try to avoid or resist any kind of demand, even if they are interested in it. PDA is often associated with autism, but it can also affect people with ADHD or other neurodiverse conditions. PDA was first proposed by Professor Elizabeth Newson in the 1980s, who observed that some autistic children had a different profile from others on the spectrum.

People with PDA may find it difficult to cope with everyday expectations and requests and may use various strategies to avoid them, such as distraction, negotiation, procrastination, or refusal. Sometimes, they may go to extreme lengths to avoid demands, such as lying, stealing, or becoming aggressive. PDA is not a deliberate choice or a sign of defiance, but rather a response to anxiety and a need for autonomy. PDA can affect both adults and children and can cause challenges in various areas of life, such as education, work, relationships, and self-care.

PDA is not officially recognised as a diagnosis by the main diagnostic manuals, such as the DSM-5-TR or the ICD-10. However, some experts and organisations consider it to be a distinct profile within the autism spectrum, with its own set of characteristics and support needs. Others argue that PDA is not a separate condition, but rather a cluster of symptoms that can be explained by other factors, such as personality traits, attachment issues, or trauma. More research is needed to understand the nature and causes of PDA, and how to best support people who experience it.

A PDA profile is not a fixed or static label, but rather a spectrum that can vary depending on various factors, such as the person's mood, environment, age, and support. Some people with a PDA profile may show more obvious or aggressive signs of demand avoidance, while others may be more subtle or passive in their resistance. A PDA profile is not a diagnosis by itself, but rather a part of the autism spectrum that requires a different approach and understanding.

I do not know if this is linked but researching PDA brought up some memories of odd made decisions, I made in my childhood which never made sense as an adult... well it did and it didn't... In primary school I'd lie about having homework, I'd say I got none.

Now I had no problem doing homework, I did not like the tension it caused so I didn't want to be in that situation. As an adult, I don't know why I didn't just do my homework by myself if I enjoyed it. Mystery.

Perfectionism is a type of cognitive distortion that makes a person set unrealistic standards for themselves and others. One of the common challenges faced by neurodivergent individuals is the tendency to set unrealistically high standards for themselves and to experience excessive self-criticism when they fail to meet them. This has been widely studied in psychology and has been linked to various mental health issues, such as anxiety, depression, eating disorders, and suicidal ideation. However, the question of whether neurodivergence is associated with higher levels of perfectionism than neurotypicality remains unresolved. There is some anecdotal evidence that suggests that neurodivergent people may be more prone to perfectionism due to factors such as social stigma, internalized ableism, executive dysfunction, and cognitive rigidity. However, there is a lack of empirical research that directly compares the prevalence and severity of perfectionism among different neurodivergent groups and between neurodivergent and neurotypical populations. Therefore, more systematic, and rigorous studies are needed to establish the relationship between neurodivergence and perfectionism and to explore the underlying mechanisms and moderators that may explain this association.

Perfectionism can lead to procrastination and low self-esteem, as well as increased stress and anxiety. For example, a perfectionist with ADHD may delay starting a project until the last minute because they fear they will not do it well enough, or they may spend hours checking and rechecking their work for errors. Another example is that a perfectionist with ADHD may have difficulty accepting compliments or constructive feedback because they focus on their flaws and mistakes instead of their strengths and achievements.

One possible reason for perfectionism in neurodivergent adults is that they experienced a lot of criticism and punishment as children for their symptoms.

Perfectionism may be a way of trying to avoid feeling disappointed, insecure, or embarrassed by their lack of attention to detail, which is a common characteristic for those who are neurodivergent. However, perfectionism can also make symptoms worse by creating more pressure and distraction.

Premenstrual dysphoric disorder (PMDD) is a severe form of premenstrual syndrome (PMS) that affects about 5% of women of reproductive age. PMDD causes significant emotional and physical symptoms that interfere with daily functioning and quality of life. Some of the common symptoms of PMDD include mood swings, irritability, anxiety, depression, fatigue, insomnia, headaches, bloating, and breast tenderness.

There is some evidence that PMDD and ADHD may be related or co-occur in some women. Both conditions involve dysregulation of neurotransmitters such as serotonin and dopamine, which are involved in mood regulation and executive functioning. Both conditions also have genetic and environmental risk factors. Some studies have found that women with PMDD are more likely to have ADHD than women without PMDD, and vice versa. Additionally, some women with ADHD may experience worsening of their symptoms during the premenstrual phase.

The diagnosis and treatment of PMDD and ADHD can be challenging, especially when they co-occur. It is important to consult a qualified health professional who can assess the symptoms and rule out other possible causes or comorbidities. The treatment options may include medication, psychotherapy, lifestyle changes, or a combination of these approaches. The goal of treatment is to reduce the severity and impact of the symptoms and improve the well-being and functioning of the affected women.

Procrastination, ah who doesn't procrastinate? Procrastination is a common problem for many people, especially those with ADHD. It means putting off an important task in favour of something more fun or easy, like tidying up the house or watching a show online. But why do we procrastinate? One possible reason is the wall of awful, a term coined by Jessica McCabe from "How to ADHD", a YouTube channel that offers helpful tips and insights for people with ADHD (Seriously check her out, she is incredible). The wall of awful is an emotional obstacle that blocks us from starting or completing a task because we are afraid of failing or facing negative consequences. The wall is made up of bricks that represent our past failures, rejections, criticisms, and disappointments. These bricks pile up over time and make us feel overwhelmed, hopeless, and stuck Jessica McCabe describes the wall of awful "*as an emotional barrier that grows out of repeated failure, preventing us from taking risks and initiating tasks*". Each brick in my wall consists of my fears and self-doubt. Built due to the rotation of past criticisms of my character, revolving in my head:

My methods of overcoming this wall were severely unhealthy and severely affected my emotional well-being. First is avoidance, pretending the wall does not exist, I distract myself with Netflix, other jobs, YouTube, you name it. This does not work; the wall is still there. So, the inevitable moment I must face the wall I am drowning in stress and become highly overwhelmed and become paralysed. Then bang, I explode in an emotional outburst. This results in a whole lot of self-disgust and anger. I need to find another method to face my wall. Some strategies that might help are:

Breaking down the task into smaller and more manageable steps

Setting a timer and working on the task for a short period

Rewarding ourselves for making progress or finishing the task

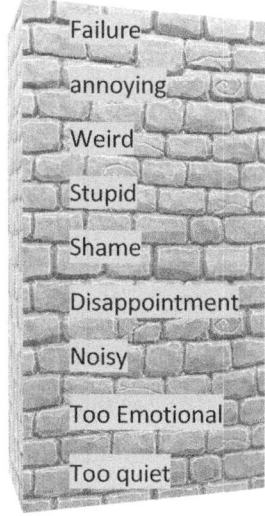

Asking for help or support from someone we trust

Challenging our negative thoughts and beliefs about ourselves and the task

Reminding ourselves of our strengths and achievements

Finding a purpose or meaning in the task

Making the task more fun or interesting

I also turned to therapy. Which is the best decision I have made. I highly recommend therapy; every individual is unique and what may work for me may not work for you.

Prosopagnosia is a neurological disorder that affects the ability to recognise and remember faces. People with prosopagnosia may rely on other cues, such as voices, clothing, or hairstyle, to identify people, but they may still struggle when these cues are absent or changed. Prosopagnosia can be acquired due to brain damage or developmentally due to genetic factors or neurodevelopmental conditions.

Autism is often associated with prosopagnosia. Several studies have suggested that prosopagnosia is more prevalent in those with Autism than in the general population, with estimates ranging from 15% to 37% of autistic adults showing impaired face recognition skills.

The link between prosopagnosia and Autism is not fully understood, but some possible explanations are:

A common genetic or neural mechanism that affects both face processing and social cognition.

A reduced exposure or interest in faces during development leads to leads to more difficulty in facial recognition later in life.

A difficulty seeing faces as a whole or finding what makes each face different.

A deficit in attention, memory, or executive functions that interferes with face recognition.

Prosopagnosia can have a significant impact on the social and emotional well-being of people with Autism, as it may impair their ability to form and maintain relationships, recognize emotions and mental states from facial expressions, and follow social cues and norms.

Therefore, it is important to identify and support individuals with Autism who have prosopagnosia, as well as to raise awareness and understanding of this condition among their families, peers, and professionals.

Rejection Sensitive Dysphoria or Rejection sensitivity? Rejection Sensitivity Dysphoria is a term created by Dr William Dodson who described it as *"a triggered, wordless emotional pain that occurs after a real or perceived loss of approval, love or respect."* According to Dr Dodson, this emotional condition can only be found in those with ADHD. However, it is not generally known among doctors or psychiatrists as it is not mentioned in the DSM-5. However, those with ADHD know it extremely well, with up to 99% of people with ADHD being more sensitive than most to rejection.

Those of us who have Rejection Sensitive Dysphoria do not handle rejection, or perceived rejection, well. It can be incredibly upsetting if someone has shunned or criticized them, even if that's not the case. The experts suspect it happens due to differences in brain structure. Those differences mean your brain can't regulate rejection-related emotions and behaviours, making them much more intense. People who have the condition sometimes work hard to make everyone like them. Or they might stop trying and stay out of any situation where they might get hurt. This social withdrawal can look like social phobia, which is a serious fear of being embarrassed in public. But most commonly there is the inability to say "No" to a situation in fear you'd be criticised, even if saying No would be best for you. This can affect relationships with family, friends, or a romantic partner.

Rejection sensitivity, on the other hand which is described as "*the tendency to anxiously expect, readily perceive, and intensely react to rejection*", is mentioned in several studies related to ADHD. Rejection sensitivity is not exclusive to ADHD but is connected to many psychiatric conditions such as social anxiety, depression, borderline personality disorder and body dysmorphia.

This is because those with ADHD have difficulty regulating emotions and have previous experience with actual rejection.

Repetitive behaviours are common symptoms of autism that can be a source of enjoyment or a way of coping with stress and sensory overload. Scientists have classified these behaviours into two types: lower-order and higher-order. Lower-order repetitive behaviours involve physical movements or vocalisations, such as hand-flapping, rocking, grunting or repeating phrases. For example, an autistic person might flap their hands when they are excited or happy, or rock back and forth when they are anxious or overwhelmed. These are also known as stimming or self-stimulating behaviours.

Higher-order repetitive behaviours involve cognitive patterns or interests, such as following routines and rituals, insisting on sameness and having intense or narrow interests. For example, an autistic person might follow the same schedule every day, get upset by any changes or disruptions, or have a deep fascination with a specific topic, such as trains, dinosaurs, or maps. These behaviours may help autistic people to feel calm, happy, and focused, but they may also limit their social opportunities, learning and flexibility, or cause distress or anxiety.

Routines and Rituals help autistic individuals feel less stressed and better able to cope with their surroundings.

Routines serve an important function by introducing order, structure and predictability which can help to manage anxiety. Because of this, it can be very distressing if a person's routine is disrupted. Sometimes minor changes such as moving between two activities can be distressing; for others, big events like holidays, birthdays, or Christmas, which create change and upheaval, can cause anxiety. Unexpected changes are often the most difficult to deal with. Some people with autism have daily timetables so that they know what is going to happen and when.

Some of the ways that routine and sameness can manifest in autistic people are:

Having rigid preferences about things like food, clothing, or everyday objects. For example, some autistic people might only eat food of a certain colour, only wear clothes made from specific fabrics, or only use particular types of soap or brands of toilet paper.

Needing routine around daily activities such as meals or bedtime. Routines can become almost ritualistic, having to be followed precisely with attention paid to the tiniest details.

Having verbal rituals, with a person repeatedly asking the same questions and needing a specific answer.

Having compulsive behaviour, for example, a person might be constantly washing their hands or checking locks. This does not necessarily mean they have obsessive-compulsive disorder (OCD) but if you are concerned about this, speak to your GP in the first instance.

Having obsessions or special interests that are very intense and focused. For example, some autistic children might collect things like twigs or balls or want to know the birthday of everyone they meet. They might open and close doors over and over again, or rush into each new place to find and flush the toilet. Older children might have very narrow interests or preoccupations, like needing to know everything possible about trains.

Dependence on routines may increase or re-emerge during adolescence. Routines can have a profound effect on the lives of people with autism, their family, and carers, but it is possible to make a person less reliant on them. Anxiety appears to be the main reason why people with autism develop and maintain routines. Routines can provide a sense of order, predictability, and control in a chaotic and unpredictable world. They can also help to cope with sensory overload, social demands, and transitions. However, routines can also limit the flexibility, spontaneity, and creativity of people with autism and their families. They can interfere with learning new skills, adapting to new situations, and exploring new interests. They can also cause distress and frustration when they are disrupted or prevented by external factors. Therefore, it is important to find a balance between respecting the need for routines and encouraging more flexibility and variety in daily life.

This is possible, with proper preparation and support, it is possible to adapt to changes more effectively and confidently. Some of the strategies that can help autistic individuals prepare for and cope with changes include:

Using visual supports: Visual supports are tools that use images, symbols, words, or objects to communicate information or instructions. They can help autistic individuals understand what is happening, what is expected of them, and what they can do in different situations. For example, visual schedules can show the sequence of activities or events in a day, visual timers can show how much time is left for a task or a transition, and visual cues can remind them of the rules or expectations in a setting.

Using social stories: Social stories are short stories that describe a situation, a person's perspective, and a possible outcome. They can help autistic individuals learn about social situations, expectations, and behaviours. They can also help them anticipate and prepare for changes that may occur in their lives, such as moving to a new house, starting a new school, or meeting new people.

Using calendars: Calendars are tools that show the dates and times of events or activities. They can help autistic individuals plan and keep track of their schedules. They can also help them see when changes are going to happen and how long they will last. For example, a calendar can show when a holiday is coming up, when a school term ends, or when a doctor's appointment is scheduled.

Using gradual exposure: Gradual exposure is a technique that involves introducing a change slowly and gradually, starting from the least challenging level and increasing the difficulty over time. It can help autistic individuals get used to a change and reduce their anxiety or resistance.

Selective mutism is described as *"an anxiety disorder where a person is unable to speak in certain social situations, such as with classmates at school or to relatives they do not see very often"*. It is of course more complicated than that, and just like many disorders can be difficult to explain or fully understood unless you suffer with it yourself. It is a complex and misunderstood condition that affects people differently depending on the context and the environment. For instance, a child with selective mutism may be mute at school but be able to talk, laugh, and sing at home (I know how that feels). Some people may think that the child is choosing when to speak and when to be silent. This is not true. Selective mutism is not a voluntary behaviour, it is a psychological reaction to extreme anxiety, where the person with selective mutism freezes and may even flee if possible. Other examples of situations where a person with selective mutism may struggle to speak are ordering food at a restaurant, answering the phone, talking to a doctor or a dentist, giving a presentation, or meeting new people.

<u>Sensory processing disorder (SPD)</u> is a neurological condition that affects how the brain receives and interprets sensory information from the environment. Sensory information includes what we see, hear, smell, taste, touch, and feel inside our bodies. SPD can affect one or more senses and can cause over- or under-responsiveness to stimuli. For example, some people with SPD may find certain sounds unbearable, while others may not notice them at all. SPD can interfere with daily functioning, learning, and social interactions.

SPD is not a single disorder, but a group of related disorders that have different symptoms and causes. Some of the types of SPD are:

Sensory modulation disorder is when the brain has trouble regulating the intensity and duration of sensory input. People with this type of SPD may be hypersensitive (over-reactive), hyposensitive (under-reactive), or sensory seeking (craving more stimulation).

Sensory discrimination disorder is when the brain has trouble distinguishing between different sensory qualities, such as shapes, textures, sounds, or smells.

People with this type of SPD may have difficulty identifying objects by touch, following directions, or performing fine motor tasks.

Sensory-based motor disorder is when the brain has trouble using sensory information to plan and execute movements. People with this type of SPD may have problems with balance, coordination, posture, or motor skills.

SPD is not an officially recognised diagnosis in the DSM-5 or the ICD-11, but it is often associated with other conditions such as ASD, ADHD, or anxiety disorders. The exact causes of SPD are not fully understood, but they may involve genetic factors, prenatal or perinatal complications, or environmental influences.

The treatment for SPD usually involves occupational therapy (OT), which helps people with SPD develop skills and strategies to cope with sensory challenges. OT may include sensory integration therapy, which exposes people with SPD to various sensory stimuli in a controlled and playful way, to help them adapt and respond appropriately. OT may also include creating a sensory diet, which is a personalized plan of sensory activities that can be done at home or school to meet the individual's sensory needs.

SPD can affect people of all ages and backgrounds, but it is more common in children than adults. Some signs of SPD in children may include:

Being easily distracted or overwhelmed by noise, lights, or crowds.

Having difficulty following instructions or staying on task.

Being clumsy, uncoordinated, or slow to learn new skills.

Being fussy about clothing, food, or grooming.

Having trouble sleeping, eating, or toilet training.

Being aggressive, impulsive, or withdrawn.

Seeking or avoiding physical contact.

Having trouble making friends or expressing emotions If you suspect that you or your child has SPD, you should consult a qualified professional who can assess the symptoms and provide appropriate treatment options. SPD can be challenging to live with, but with proper support and intervention, it can be managed and overcome.

Stimming is a term that stands for self-stimulatory behaviours, which are repetitive movements or sounds that people do to regulate their emotions or sensory needs. Stimming is often associated with Autism, but it can also be in people with ADHD, OCD, schizophrenia, and other conditions.

Some common forms of stimming are hand-flapping, finger-flicking, rocking, jumping, spinning, twirling, head-banging, and complex body movements. Some people also stim by making noises, humming, singing, or repeating words or phrases. Others may stim by touching different textures, biting their nails, pulling their hair, or rubbing their fingers.

Some people may stim by looking at specific objects or watching repetitive movements.

Another form of stimming involves sound, known as vocal stimming. This is when someone makes noises with their mouth or voice to produce sensory stimulation. Vocal stimming can be done by anyone, regardless of whether they can speak or not. Some autistic people who are non-verbal, preverbal, or minimally verbal may use vocal stimming more often than others. Vocal stimming can include groaning, grunting, screeching, squealing, humming, or repeating random words or sounds. Some people may also vocalise parts of songs, movies, or videos that they like. Vocal stimming is not always related to autism. Some people with ADHD may also vocalize as a way of expressing their hyperactivity or impulsivity. For example, they may blurt out things without thinking, hum when they are bored, or sing along to a catchy tune. These behaviours may be seen as symptoms of ADHD by the National Institute of Mental Health (NIMH).

Stimming can have different purposes and functions for different people. Some people may stim to help them focus and control their impulses, while others may stim to relieve their anxiety and calm themselves down. For example, a person with ADHD may stim by tapping their foot or fidgeting with a toy to help them concentrate on a task. While a person with ASD may stim by rocking or humming to calm themselves down when they feel overwhelmed by their environment. Personally, finger flicking is my go-to stim, it is my excited stim, I rock side to side when I am feeling content, calm yet alert, and I rock back and forth when negatively stimulated, usually just before a meltdown or during.

However, not everyone who stims has a disorder, stimming is a normal human behaviour that can be seen in anyone. For instance, some people may twirl their hair or doodle when they are nervous or bored. Stimming only becomes a problem when it interferes with daily functioning or causes harm to oneself or others.

Some researchers have suggested that the term 'stimming' may be problematic because it implies that the behaviours are merely self-stimulatory and do not have any other meaning or function. They argue that this may lead to misunderstanding and stigmatisation of people who stim and may also prevent them from exploring alternative ways of expressing themselves or coping with their challenges.

One of the ways to support people who stim is to understand why they do it and what they are trying to achieve. Another way is to accept them for who they are and respect their choices.

Stimming is not a bad thing that requires management. It is a natural and healthy way of coping and expressing oneself. However, some forms of stimming can be harmful or disruptive to oneself or others. For example, head-banging can cause injury, while loud vocalisations can disturb other people. In these cases, it may be helpful to find alternative ways of stimming that is safer and more appropriate for the situation.

If you are a parent and wonder if you should let your child stim, it depends on the type and frequency of the stimming behaviour. If the stimming is harmless and does not interfere with your child's learning, socializing, or daily functioning, you may not need to intervene.

However, if the stimming is dangerous or disruptive, you may want to seek professional help and guidance on how to manage it.

The benefits of autistic stimming can be associated with a reduction in over or under-stimulation, regulating emotions, and reducing pain. Engaging in these positive coping strategies can reduce the destructive and potentially harmful reactions that can appear when we are unable to self-regulate. Punishing stimming behaviour will not eliminate the behaviour. If anything, it can cause the behaviour to be replaced with more severe or harmful behaviour. As Dr. Heller a clinical psychologist states *"The idea that you can harness fidgeting to improve focus may be somewhat new and some people may view it as unconventional. Nonetheless, as a clinical psychologist, I have seen first-hand countless times the real impact that harnessing fidgeting can have on people of all ages in improving focus."* Stimming is a natural and normal part of being autistic. It is not something to be ashamed of or punished for. Rather, it is something to be understood and respected. By supporting autistic people's stimming needs and preferences, we can help them thrive and flourish in their unique ways.

Synaesthesia is a perceptual phenomenon that involves a cross-wiring of the senses, such that stimulation of one sense leads to involuntary experiences in another sense.

For example, some synesthetes may see colours when they hear sounds, or taste flavours when they read words. Synaesthesia is not a disorder, but rather a variation of human perception that affects about 4% of the population.

There are many different types of synaesthesia. The most common type is grapheme-colour synaesthesia, in which letters and numbers have specific colours associated with them. Another common type is chromesthesia, in which sounds trigger visual sensations of colours and shapes.

There are many types of synaesthesia, depending on which senses are involved. The most common type is grapheme-colour synaesthesia, in which letters and numbers have specific colours, and chromesthesia, in which sounds, and music evoke colours or shapes. Some synesthetes may also experience spatial-sequence synaesthesia, in which numbers, dates, or other sequences have fixed locations in space. Synaesthetes usually experience their sensations internally, in their mind's eye, but some may project them externally as if they were real objects in space. Synaesthesia is not a form of hallucination, but a consistent and involuntary association that does not interfere with normal perception. Synaesthetes often report that their condition enhances their memory, creativity, and aesthetic appreciation.

One of the rarest forms of synaesthesia is lexical-gustatory synaesthesia, in which spoken and written language (as well as some colours and emotions) causes individuals to experience an automatic and highly consistent taste or smell. This type of synaesthesia affects only about 0.2% of synaesthetes. Lexical-gustatory synaesthetes may find some words delicious and others disgusting, depending on their associations. Another interesting form of synaesthesia is tactile-emotional synaesthesia, in which looking at certain objects or people can trigger a physical sensation on the skin, such as warmth, coldness, pressure or pain. This type of synaesthesia is more common among autistic individuals than among the general population.

Synaesthesia is believed to be caused by increased connectivity between different brain regions that process sensory information. It is usually present from birth or early childhood and tends to run in families.

Synaesthesia can have both advantages and disadvantages for the people who experience it. Some benefits may include enhanced memory, creativity, and artistic abilities. Some challenges may include sensory overload, confusion, or difficulty with certain tasks.

Synaesthesia is a fascinating topic that has attracted the interest of many researchers, artists, and writers. Some famous people who have or have had synaesthesia include Vincent van Gogh, Vladimir Nabokov, Pharrell Williams, and Billie Eilish. Synaesthesia can also be simulated or induced by drugs, meditation, hypnosis, or brain stimulation. However, these are not the same as the natural and consistent experiences of synesthetes.

Studies published in 2013 one led by Simon Baron-Cohen and another by Janina Neufeld determined that approximately 20% of people with Autism Spectrum Disorder have synaesthesia. Suggesting a link between these two conditions. In addition, Vanessa van Leeuwen and colleagues in 2020 found when autism and synaesthesia co-occur in the same individual, the chance of developing heightened cognitive and memory abilities is increased.

Synaesthesia is a fascinating phenomenon that reveals the diversity and complexity of human perception. It is not yet fully understood how synaesthesia develops or what causes it, but it likely involves both genetic and environmental factors. Synaesthesia can be seen as a gift that enriches one's sensory experience and cognitive abilities.

Theory of mind is "*the cognitive capacity to think about mental states, including emotions, beliefs, desires, and knowledge, both our own and of others. It is not only thinking about thinking, but also predicting or explaining behaviour based on our guesses. Without this ability, we would not be able to understand people well enough to have proper social interactions and reciprocal conversations."*

As stated by Atsushi Senju in their 2012 paper, this ability is crucial for the development of social communication, which is characterised by profound difficulties in social interaction and communication. Theory of mind allows us to understand that other people have different beliefs, desires, emotions, and knowledge from our own, and to predict and interpret their behaviour accordingly.

ToM is important for social communication and interaction, as it helps us to predict and explain other people's behaviour and to empathise with them.

Research has shown that individuals on the Autism spectrum may have difficulty developing ToM, which can lead to challenges with social skills, repetitive behaviours, and nonverbal communication.

One of the ways researchers use to test ToM is using false-belief tasks, which require the understanding that someone can have a belief that is different from reality and one's own belief. An example of theory of mind is the classic false-belief task, the Sally-Anne task which tests whether a child can understand that another person's belief may not match reality. One version of this task involves two dolls, Sally and Anne, and a ball. Sally is playing with the ball, which she places in a basket before leaving the room to go to the bathroom. In her absence, Anne takes the ball from the basket and places it in a box. After a time, Sally comes back to the room and wants to play with the ball. Where will she look for it? To have a theory of mind, Sally would look for it in the basket (and not in the box, where it now is) because that's where she placed it. However, without a theory of mind, one cannot imagine that Sally's knowledge differs from their own. They would say that Sally would look for it in the box.

Studies have found that many children with Autism fail false-belief tasks, suggesting they have impaired ToM. However, some individuals with Autism can pass false-belief tests, but they may still struggle with more complex ToM tasks that require reasoning through a problem or understanding emotions. Some researchers believe that mind-blindness, or a lack of ToM, is present in all people on the autism spectrum due to neurological differences.

However, ToM is not a unitary concept, and different aspects of ToM are affected differently in Autism. For example, some researchers have proposed that two types of ToM exist: cognitive ToM and affective ToM. Cognitive ToM refers to the ability to infer what others think or know, while affective ToM refers to the ability to infer what others feel or desire. Some studies have suggested that individuals with Autism may have more difficulties with affective ToM than cognitive ToM.

Moreover, ToM is not a static trait, but a dynamic process that depends on the context and the interaction partner. Some researchers have argued that ToM is not only a problem for individuals with Autism, but also for neurotypical individuals who interact with them. This is known as the double empathy problem, which suggests that both groups may have trouble understanding each other's perspective and communication styles. Therefore, ToM may not be a deficit in Autism, but a difference that requires mutual adaptation and respect.

Time Blindness means you have trouble perceiving and managing time accurately, and this is a common cognitive difficulty seen in many ADHDers. Time blindness can affect the ability to plan, prioritise, and complete tasks, as well as their punctuality and sense of how long things take. Time blindness are problems with attention, memory, impulse control, executive functions, and dopamine levels in the brain. People with ADHD also tend to have a disrupted circadian rhythm, which makes it harder to adjust to the natural cycles of day and night. Time blindness can negatively impact the academic, occupational, and social functioning of people with ADHD. However, some strategies can help them cope with time blindness, such as using medication, visual timers, schedules, breaks, apps, and the double-time principle. By understanding how ADHD affects their perception of time and applying these techniques, people with ADHD can improve their time management skills and reduce their stress levels.

Common Learning difficulties as comorbidities of ADHD and Autism:

Learning disabilities are a term that covers various disorders that affect how a person learns, understands, or uses information. They are not a reflection of you or your child's intelligence or how hard you are trying. A popular way to describe Learning Disabilities is that your brain is wired differently, and you receive and process information differently.

Learning disabilities can make reading, writing, spelling, and math difficult. They can affect your ability to organise and recall information, your ability to listen and speak, and can impact your short-term and long-term memory and timing.

The term learning disabilities is a collective term for a range of specific learning challenges. Learning disabilities are not problems with learning due to vision or hearing problems.

Developmental Language Disorder (DLD) is a neurodevelopmental condition that affects the acquisition and use of language in children and adults. DLD is not caused by hearing impairment, intellectual disability, autism spectrum disorder, or brain injury, although it may co-occur with these conditions. DLD is estimated to affect 7% of the population, making it more common than dyslexia or autism. However, DLD is often under-recognized and underdiagnosed, leading to difficulties in accessing appropriate support and services. DLD is a form of neurodivergence, which means that the brains of people with DLD process information differently from the typical or expected way. DLD is not something to be cured or fixed, but rather to be understood and respected. People with DLD and other neurodivergent conditions have the right to be included and supported in all aspects of life, such as education, employment, health care, and social relationships. They also have the right to express their identity and preferences, and to participate in decisions that affect them. By recognizing and celebrating neurodiversity, we can create a more inclusive and equitable society for everyone.

Dyscalculia is a learning disorder that affects a person's ability to understand number-based information and math. People who have dyscalculia struggle with numbers and math because their brains don't process math-related concepts like the brains of people without this disorder. Dyscalculia is sometimes called "numbers dyslexia," but this is misleading because dyslexia refers to difficulty reading and writing, while dyscalculia is specifically related to mathematics.

Some of the common symptoms of dyscalculia include:

Difficulty understanding or remembering mathematical concepts such as multiplication, division, fractions, carrying, and borrowing.

Difficulty reconciling verbal or written cues (such as the word "two") and their math symbols and signifiers (the number 2).

Trouble explaining math processes or showing work when asked to complete a mathematical task.

Difficulty describing the sequence of events or remembering the steps in a math process.

People with dyscalculia may also have trouble with:

Understanding numbers. Either their magnitude or relationship with one another. (Typical dyscalculia example: $5*6= x, x= 56$).

Number sense - understanding of how numbers work, numerical values and how to compare or estimate quantities on a number line.

Understanding fractions. As well as basic math

operations patterns.

Putting language into the math process is very hard to implement.

Making a change or handling money.

Mathematical reasoning. It is a hard pattern to follow since the basic understanding of math is hard to master.

Manipulating numbers or solving math problems is very hard for them, almost impossible.

Inability to read graphs and charts.

As a result, they struggle to memorize math facts-formulas, equations, and text assignments. Since they don't understand the logic underlying the steps involved in math operations, they must rely on rote memorization i.e., learning through repetition. All these difficulties cause long-term problems with math operations such as addition, subtraction, multiplication, and division.

The exact causes of dyscalculia are not well understood, but some possible factors include:

-Lack of concrete early instruction in mathematics. Children who are taught that math concepts are simply a series of conceptual rules to follow, instead of being instructed in the hands-on reasoning behind those rules, may not develop the neural pathways they need to understand more complicated mathematical frameworks.

-Genetic factors. Mathematical aptitude tends to run in families, as do learning disabilities. However, it's hard to tell how much aptitude is hereditary and how much is the result of family culture.

-Coexisting conditions. Dyscalculia may occur by itself, or it may occur alongside other developmental delays and neurological conditions such as dyslexia, ADHD, depression, and anxiety.

Dyscalculia can be diagnosed by a qualified professional such as a psychologist or an educational specialist who can administer standardized tests and observe the person's performance in math-related tasks. The diagnosis process may also involve interviews with the person and their family members, teachers, or employers to get a comprehensive picture of their strengths and weaknesses in math.

There is no cure for dyscalculia, but there are ways to help people with this disorder improve their math skills and cope with their challenges. Some possible interventions include:

Individualized instruction that focuses on the person's specific needs and learning style. This may involve using concrete materials such as manipulatives, visual aids, or games to illustrate math concepts and make them more engaging and meaningful.

Accommodations that reduce the stress and anxiety associated with math tasks. This may include allowing extra time, using calculators or other tools, providing written instructions or examples, breaking down complex problems into smaller steps or allowing alternative ways of demonstrating knowledge such as oral or written responses.

Cognitive behavioural therapy (CBT) helps the person develop positive attitudes and strategies towards math and overcome negative emotions such as fear, frustration, or shame. CBT can also help the person cope with coexisting conditions such as depression or anxiety that may affect their motivation and self-esteem.

Support from family members, teachers or peers who can provide encouragement, feedback, and guidance. They can also help the person apply their math skills to real-life situations and appreciate the relevance and usefulness of math in everyday life.

Dyscalculia can be a challenging condition that affects many aspects of a person's life, but it does not mean that they are less intelligent or less capable than others. With proper diagnosis, intervention and support, people with dyscalculia can overcome their difficulties and achieve their goals in math and beyond.

Dysgraphia is a condition that affects a person's ability to write. It is not related to intelligence, vision, or reading skills. People with dysgraphia may have problems with:

Spelling words correctly and consistently.

Writing legibly and neatly.

-Using proper grammar and punctuation.

-Aligning letters and words on the page.

-Holding and controlling the writing instrument.

-Visualizing how to form letters and words.

-Expressing their thoughts in writing.

These difficulties can make writing a slow and frustrating task for people with dysgraphia. They may also experience fatigue, cramps, or pain in their hand or arm while writing. Their writing may lack clarity and coherence, and they may avoid writing tasks whenever possible.

Dysgraphia can be caused by different factors, such as problems with working memory, orthographic coding, language processing, or fine motor skills. It can also result from a brain injury or a stroke that damages the part of the brain responsible for writing. Dysgraphia can occur alone or along with other learning differences, such as dyslexia or autism.

Dysgraphia can be diagnosed by a professional who can assess the person's writing skills and identify the areas of weakness. Some interventions can help people with dysgraphia improve their writing abilities, such as:

Using assistive technology, such as speech-to-text software, word processors, or graphic organizers.

Practicing handwriting skills with different tools and techniques, such as pencil grips, slant boards, tracing, or copying.

Learning strategies to plan, organize, and revise their writing.

Getting feedback and support from teachers, tutors, or peers.

Dysgraphia is a lifelong condition that can affect a person's academic, professional, and personal life. However, with proper diagnosis and treatment, people with dysgraphia can overcome their challenges and develop their writing skills.

Dyslexia is a learning difference that affects how people process language, especially reading, spelling, and writing. It is estimated that about 10% of the population has some degree of dyslexia. Dyslexia is not a sign of low intelligence or laziness. It is a lifelong condition that can be managed with appropriate strategies and support. People with dyslexia have diverse strengths and challenges and may excel in areas such as creativity, problem-solving, or oral communication.

Dyspraxia is a term that describes a condition that affects the ability to plan and execute movements, especially those that require fine motor skills, language, and planning abilities. Dyspraxia is also known as developmental coordination disorder (DCD) or clumsy child syndrome. Dyspraxia is not a learning difficulty, but it can make learning certain skills more challenging. Dyspraxia can often co-occur with ADHD and Autism, but they are separate conditions. Dyspraxia does not affect intelligence, but it can affect coordination skills, such as balancing, playing sports, or driving a car.

I wanted to end this chapter by leaving you with the knowledge that Learning disabilities are not a sign of low intelligence or laziness. They are simply differences in how the brain processes information. However, many people with learning disabilities struggle with low self-esteem because they face academic challenges, social stigma, and negative feedback from others. This can affect their mental health and well-being. If you have a learning disability and ADHD/Autism, you may face additional difficulties in learning and demonstrating your knowledge in the traditional format. You may also have trouble with attention, organization, communication, or social skills. These challenges can make you feel frustrated, isolated, or inadequate.

However, having a learning disability and

ADHD/Autism does not mean you cannot succeed in school or life. You have many strengths and abilities that can help you overcome your challenges. You also have the right to receive support and accommodation that suit your learning style and needs. You are not alone; many people understand and appreciate you for who you are.

It is normal to feel emotional when writing or talking about your learning disability and ADHD/Autism. It can be hard to accept and embrace your differences, especially when you face obstacles or discrimination.

However, it is important to recognise and celebrate your achievements, talents, and passions. You are a valuable and unique person who deserves respect and happiness.

Chapter 4:
My Childhood

I do believe taking the plunge and searching for an answer was the best decision I've made for myself, just for the answers this diagnosis provided; things make more sense, not everything, and it's not the answer to everything, but there is a definite positive sense of self I did not have before. I finally understand more about who I am and what makes me this way. It has been very interesting and illuminating to look back at my childhood with a new lens and mindset. I always felt different from my peers, as if I was behind a glass wall with no way to their side, just watching everyone making these connections, I had the wrong key, which did not fit the lock. I had my way of thinking and doing things, but it could be quite isolating. Looking back, I see an amalgamation of both ADHD and Autism traits strewn throughout my life like breadcrumbs left to lead me to the answers I was looking for.

As I mentioned in Chapter 1 the phrase "a bit autistic" was said light-heartedly throughout my life. I just accepted it, no questions asked or searching for answers (which is not like me at all), this comment would usually be followed by "But everyone's a bit autistic", which made me more confused, if everyone's a bit autistic why I am the only one being singled out (Now this could be rejection sensitivity poking its little head). ADHD on the other hand had never been on my radar. It came up in conversation twice in my life but never concerning myself. This would be why, finally, in November 2022, I started looking into Autism, to get an eventual autism assessment. In my research, it appeared that many of the traits associated with autism did not apply to me.

Specifically, delayed speech as a child. I was speaking in full sentences before I turned 18 months old. Even a public health nurse stated that I could not be autistic due to my early speech development. It was only later, after my ADHD diagnosis, that I found out that delayed speech is not the norm in girls with autism. I learned this while watching a presentation by Sarah Hendrix sent to me by my psychiatrist. Sarah Hendrix is an autistic woman who shared her experiences growing up as a girl with autism (I will list all the sources I used for this book at the end). I was amazed by how much I related to her story. She had similar special interests as me, such as Pokémon, horses, and rabbits. She also explained that delayed speech is not as common in girls with autism as it is in boys. Girls with autism tend to be very verbal and articulate, but this can mask their underlying communication difficulties.

However, I am getting ahead of myself, in chapter 1 I go into what brought me to an ADHD diagnosis, and the TedTalks that were an eye opener. In one of the TedTalks Jessica McCabe talked about how she was talking in full sentences at 18 months old, how she was a quiet daydreamer and spent most of her time reading, where most of her friends were found in these books.

Losing things constantly and if she had to concentrate on anything she was not interested in was like "nailing jello to the wall". With every word she said I nodded in agreement non-stop.

I connected so viscerally to both of these women's stories, they could provide me with a detailed description of how I felt. I had the words to describe me and how I thought and where I struggled.

This chapter, as promised, will now go into my childhood, and how I now understand my behaviours and tics. I'll start with "concentration" as that is where my first memories stem and it was my concentration which provided the first clues. I was interested in learning from a very young age, I wanted to know everything, and I wanted to do everything. I could speak some Irish and French quite young, my mother was great at keeping me motivated and entertained at home. However, creche or play school was a different matter, it was so tedious and dull in comparison. I refused to get involved in nursery songs or rhymes. Instead, I would just drift off into a daydream. Even when my grandmother sang "clap hands clap hands" to me in my buggy, I would not acknowledge her. She of course became very concerned, asking my grandfather "What's wrong with her?", he took one look at me, and connected the dots immediately pointing up and saying, "It's the birds!". It was my grandfather who taught me all about the garden birds, flowers, and insects as I followed him around the garden as he worked. I'm getting tears in my eyes writing this, I have such fond memories of that time, I can still smell his greenhouse when I think of this time.

Thus, it should not surprise you very much that my special interests, now and in childhood were and is animals and nature. This meant I spent much of my time watching birds, ants, and bees (absolutely love bees, amazing animals) and completely shut out everything else outside that. This would also mean to my mother's dismay, the attraction of these animals to me… and not just the birds, I would try to hand feed the ants… maybe it was good it was just ants. Once I got a microscope, I started to bring little bits of nature inside, spending hours observing leaves, insects, soil, and puddle water under the microscope lens.

When I was not outside, I would be creating characters and worlds in my notebooks. However, I often lost interest before I even really started the plot. And these characters would continue their life in my head, I had a vivid imagination and spent a lot of time daydreaming. These daydreams were like movies and incredibly intricate, I would look forward to the time I could escape to them. I would escape to this fantasy world at night or during school. School is not the best choice I know, and when caught my teacher would be understandably annoyed with me for being distracted. Annoyingly while these daydreams were so detailed and played like a movie I was cast in, I struggled to get them onto paper and never followed through. Maybe someday. I still remember every scene in detail.

As I mentioned above, my siblings and I were granted every opportunity to be creative at home. I was never bored; our mom encouraged our creativity and if we did happen to utter those 3 words "I am bored", we were given a project on Rome or Egypt, dinosaurs, or sharks. We had access to books, art supplies (paint, crayons, pencils, Play-Doh and more), and copybooks for writing.

Our interests were always nurtured, my uncle and aunt gave me so many National Geographic magazines from the 90s, videos, and a book on almost every vertebrate animal (I miss that book, it was incredible. And Huge). I also received a microscope for Christmas (twice as one broke), a chemistry set and rock sets. Creche or preschool was extremely dull in comparison. My mom even tried to enrol me in a Montessori, but they said I was too young. She would always thrive for the best for me and my siblings. When my sister and I developed a passion for horses, she found a stable that accepted younger children, and Dad drove us all over the country to compete. That experience taught me something that I may never fully understand. Something about horses is magic. They have a way of soothing our stresses, easing our worries, and boosting our confidence. My mum must have known this, even though she often joked that she was crazy for letting us ride.

Now I would like to go into my interests which I was a bit more private about, especially when I got older: Pokémon and Beyblades. Pokémon interestingly is one of the topics of interest considered quite common in girls with Autism. Girls' special interests tend to include TV shows, actors, or music which are generally deemed more socially acceptable than boys' interests which may include schedules, statistics, or transportation. Saying that I love statistics. Girls' special interests may be deemed more socially acceptable to an extent, it is the intensity of the interest, however, which veers from the norm. So, it was here I went to Bing AI for an example, and what it came up with is exactly me. This is what Bing had to say *"For example, a girl who loves horses might spend hours reading about them, drawing them, and talking about them non-stop. She might know everything there is to know about different breeds, colours, and personalities of horses. She might even pretend to be a horse herself, galloping around the playground and neighing at her classmates. This kind of behaviour might seem cute or quirky at first, but it can also isolate her from her peers and make her a target for bullying. Autistic girls may struggle to balance their passion with social expectations, and may feel pressured to hide or suppress their interests in order to fit in."* I wasn't the horse, I had a team of 4 imaginary horses, I wrote their names, breeds, colours, and ages on a sheet of note paper which was then laminated (with sellotape). I was a perfectionist as a child and liked to have everything in order. This seems to be a common trait among neurodivergent individuals, who may face more challenges with social stigma, internalized ableism, executive dysfunction, and cognitive rigidity. However, the empirical support for this observation is limited. In my case, whenever I had to clean the house, I would spend a lot of time making sure that every spot was spotless, sanitising the bathroom, vacuuming the stairs, or sweeping the floor until there was no trace of dust, which could take hours. In addition, I would regularly perform categorisation behaviour, I would sort things by colour or size, such as coins, clothes, CDs, books, and stationery. I was told I was a bit OCD (Obsessive Compulsive Disorder), but this was not the case. I just need to clarify that; I did not make deals or create scenarios for fear something bad would happen if I did not create order. There was comfort in the organisation, it brought peace and relaxation. This habit did sometimes cause me some trouble in class, due to me taking so long to set up or pack up my things. This led to me often hearing "Laura are you with us?" or "Laura are you ready?" from my teachers.

So unsurprisingly, I was quite a solitary child who enjoyed playing alone or reading alone more than spending time with others. Although I did sometimes play with others, I mostly hung out with boys who shared my hobbies. I was very adventurous and energetic, and I loved to run, climb, and explore new places. As I stated above, I loved Pokémon and Beyblades, and it was boys who liked them too, I'd spend hours having battles with them. But Beyblades were more than just toys to me. There was a comfort in the shape and weight of them, I would customise them to fit the aesthetic I liked. When I was young, nobody minded that. But as I got older, I became more secretive about it. I didn't want anyone at school to know that I played with Beyblades, although I didn't have any friends there so that wasn't a problem. I generally just played with my brother's friends, who were four years younger than me, they didn't seem to care about age just that they were getting to play. I loved Pokémon, I liked to sort them by types, moves, and levels. I would write down all this information on a piece of paper and laminate it with tape. I would keep this paper with me all the time and create daydreams of the adventures we were going on.

While I loved to climb and run around, I was not always the most graceful child. I must say, one benefit of horse riding was improving balance. I had poor proprioception, which meant I was clumsy and awkward. I would constantly bump into things and my weird gait caused me to knock my ankles together, causing them to bleed. The scabs never healed because when they came close, I would hit them again and again and the scabs would reopen. I found this extremely irritating and tried to protect my ankles, usually just covering them with socks. My husband calls me the most coordinated clumsy person he has ever seen. I can move with elegance in some situations but then trip over nothing. I often spill water or coffee on myself, leaving me with a wet cold, or hot then cold lap.

Sensory over and under stimulation were also very common, I could never verbalise what I was experiencing and usually just resulted in rare outbursts. I am only now understanding what I was experiencing, and the causes after I got diagnosed. Overstimulation is caused by different things, such as touch, noise, smells, and emotions. Touch was a big issue for me, I hate light touches on my skin, whether from people or clothes. I needed to wear clothes that felt good on my body, either light and airy or pressure on certain parts of my body. I liked long dresses, leggings, and oversized jumpers with soft fabrics. But I also liked tight belts around my waist and jeans with the right texture. I didn't care about fashion or style at all. The only pair of heels I owned for maybe two long were quite comfortable and the right height, I wore them until they fell apart. When someone touched me lightly, I would feel it for a long time, and it would make me anxious and tense until the sensation faded away.

Learning about my sensitivity to noise and smells was a very "oh of course" moment. The extent they could affect my mood was huge and could make me extremely overwhelmed. I did not like the loud noises produced by trains or car washes, I had to be outside the car while it was being washed. I also hated smells that were all combined like garbage (while the smell of stagnant water was fine), The smell of certain alcohols, and plants was also incredibly uncomfortable, they made me feel sick and anxious. But with this new knowledge, I also discovered some things that helped me calm down. For example, the warmth of the sun on my skin or the smell of peppermint and chamomile, makes me feel relaxed and happy and could completely shut down an incoming meltdown due to overstimulation.

Emotional Dysregulation is extremely common in Individuals with ADHD and/or Autism. I have always been a very emotional person, and I feel things very deeply. Sometimes this can be overwhelming for me and others, especially when I see something unfair or cruel happening. For example, when I watch a movie where someone is being bullied, I get very upset and angry. I would even shout "LEAVE HIM ALONE" at the screen or just burst into dramatic hyperventilating tears out of nowhere. My mother told me that I have had a strong sense of justice ever since I was a child. I would not tolerate any harm to people or living things, even tiny bugs like clover mites. I once tried to pop the tires of some kids who were squashing them, but I failed. I know that many autistic people and ADHDers share this trait of being sensitive to injustice, even if it doesn't affect them personally. I also have trouble watching movies where friends betray each other. It makes me feel sick and sad. Recently, I went through a rough patch because I kept seeing negative videos on my feed. They made me feel hopeless and depressed. I didn't understand why they affected me so much, and I had to work with my therapist to overcome it. It took me five days to return to normal.

One of the problems with feeling all this intense emotion and overstimulation was not knowing what I was feeling, why and how to explain it. Injustice was clear and I had a target. But most of the time it was not very clear, such as the above examples of sensory issues. My mum used to tell me I needed to talk about how I felt more… This was extremely confusing to me; I had no idea how to do that and had no idea what she meant. Then I learnt about Alexithymia, which is the trouble understanding and expressing your own emotions.

Another eye-opener was learning about mirror-touch synaesthesia. This means I feel a similar sensation on the same (or opposite) part of the body that another person feels, and I can also feel the emotions of other people as if they were my own, I pick up the positive and negative emotions in others. This results in me being extremely anxious, stressed and confused during a lot of my childhood. Not understanding what I'm feeling and why, and not being able to explain how I am feeling, would result in intense migraines which can last days. But on the positive side, if someone is happy, I see an eruption of colour, and I feel extreme excitement and joy. I thought I only had the emotional component of mirror-touch synaesthesia, but I now realise I also had a touch component, especially when someone was in pain it was not as strong. When my sister complained about being sore somewhere, I would say "Wow me too". It drove her mad as she thought I was copying her, and trying to annoy her, I wasn't intentionally. I did feel the discomfort. It's kind of funny thinking about this now and receiving so many "Ah-Ha" moments.

One of the ways I was unconsciously coping with the

sensory overload I experienced was by engaging in some repetitive behaviours (stims). My stimming repertoire includes finger tapping or hand movements, fingerpicking, rocking back and forth or side to side, mouth movements, and humming all of which help me regulate my nervous system. My most common stims were finger tapping, which I generally carried out when excited, and positively overstimulated. I rocked side to side when I was calm, while back and forth rocking I was always alone and extremely negatively overwhelmed. The two stims I tried to conceal or minimise because I didn't want anyone to notice them were the stroking of my hand, arm, or palm, I hated being touched by others, but I found it soothing to touch my skin. Nail picking however was the one I was teased about; I tend to do this when I was nervous. I was in a pony camp and a group of kids around my age or younger were following me copying me and making weird noises. I pretended to be sick and didn't return until the last day.

Another new term I learnt through my diagnosis was Interoception and issues related to struggling with this, this was present throughout my life. Interoception is the sense that helps us feel what is happening inside our body, such as our heartbeat, breathing, hunger signs, thirst, pain, and emotions. A person with interoceptive issues have trouble sensing or interpreting these signals from their body. This can affect our physical and mental health in various ways. For example, I have a hyposensitivity to pain, which means I don't feel pain as much as other people do. This is because of my interoceptive issues. Saying I have a high pain threshold is an understatement, I don't notice when something is wrong with my body until it becomes very serious, and my body just says nope. This has led to some medical emergencies in the past, such as pneumonia, septicaemia, rheumatic fever, appendix rupture and ectopic pregnancy. All of these were caused by my not noticing the symptoms, from a sore throat to a ruptured fallopian tube. I need be very careful and check my body regularly for any signs of internal injury or illness.

However, having a high pain threshold was helpful when I gave birth to my son. I enjoyed the process, and it was very calming. I only used gas and air for some extra relief and that was fun. The one problem was the cue to push was confusing.

Other examples of interoceptive issues are having trouble knowing when I am hungry or full, hot, or cold, thirsty, or hydrated, or needing to use the bathroom. These can affect my eating habits, hydration levels, body temperature regulation, and bladder control. But I am learning more about them and how to cope with them. Some strategies can help me improve my interoception and awareness of my body's signals. For example:

- Practicing mindfulness meditation and Pilates can help me focus on my breathing and sensations in different parts of my body.

- Using a journal and having a set time to eat helps me track my mood, hunger, thirst, pain, and other bodily states throughout the day.

- Asking for feedback from others mainly my husband, can help me validate and understand my feelings and experiences better.

- Seeking professional help from a doctor or a therapist has helped me manage any physical or mental health issues that may be related to my interoception.

Interoception is an important but often overlooked sense that shapes our well-being. By learning more about this and its effects, I believe I can improve my quality of life and happiness.

Now I may say I have an extremely high pain threshold; migraines are a different story entirely. This is one kind of pain that I cannot handle at all. It is usually caused by being overstimulated by my hypersensitivities. These can trigger a migraine attack. These migraines came into their own during my adolescence. I did not do well as a teenage girl. I had completely missed that line between childhood and adolescence, it was not clear to me at all. Suddenly, I was in Secondary school and the rules had changed, these new rules were confusing, and the social cues were tedious. None of it made sense to me. To try and pass off at least somewhat relatable, I would study the characters in movies and tv shows, taking their mannerisms, phrases, and even facial expressions. Then I'd go to a mirror and practice the faces, replay their words in my head, creating scripted scenarios, and potential conversational outcomes, and just run them over and over. This didn't help at all; real life is nothing like the movies. And people do not generally talk in this manner, most of the time I just did not talk to anyone and kept to myself (I will go into more detail in Chapter 5 on education). What didn't help was the country of origin of these shows, I mostly watched American movies and tv shows to learn how to act. My mom and sister would make direct comments about me sounding American. "Stop saying that you sound American" was said daily.

It was during my teenage years I struggled with eye contact; I do not have much memory of struggling with this in primary school. It was physically impossible to look into someone's eyes at this time. The only time I felt an improvement was when I moved to Dublin to start school at the Institute of Education, I'll get to that in the next chapter.

There is only one regret I've had of a late diagnosis, and that is squashing my creativity (which has very little to do with my diagnosis really). I stopped drawing, and writing fictional stories as it did not appear to be a socially acceptable pastime in some circles. I had not properly daydreamed or created a story in years. I had not drawn, painted or even attempted a work of fiction for maybe 15 years. I had even reduced my reading for relaxation. Never give up on your special interest, there is nothing wrong with them. Now I am going back to what I love, that is my one regret.

I will end this chapter with four self-affirmations to always keep in mind:

I am not defective, I am different.

I am a good and interesting person. I will accept myself for who I am. I will rejoice in my uniqueness.

These affirmations are based on some of the ones suggested by OptimistMinds for autistic people. They can help you boost your self-esteem and confidence and remind you of your strengths and gifts. You can repeat them daily or whenever you need a positive boost.

Chapter 5
My Education

7 years ago, ADHD was referred to as a Disruptive Behaviour problem and considered a bad thing. It still has a lot of stigma which is in definite need to change, I'm hoping this book will help educate with stories, but we shall see... It was these "Disruptive" behaviours that were targeted for treatment due to them being deemed a problem. It was believed that if these behaviours were terminated, we would do better in school and make more friends. Not surprisingly ADHD does not work that way. Turns out there's a lot more to ADHD than just being hyper and impulsive. And some of us do not present in that way. We just appear to be lost in our thoughts or bored by the same old stuff. But the teachers don't tend to notice that. They only saw the loud ones.

And then there's Autism, which was and still is quite understood, understanding is growing every day I must say but what is learned is not common knowledge. People with autism were often labelled as weird, defective, or even dangerous. As Autism was just considered a matter of being socially inept, emotionally detached or intellectually impaired. So, discrimination, exclusion and abuse are present in many aspects of their lives. They didn't realize that some of us just have a different way of seeing, hearing, and feeling the world. That some of us needed more time and space to process things and that we have special interests and talents that make us happy, and we don't need to be ashamed of them.

Things have changed a bit since then, but not enough. In 2019, a charity called AsIAm surveyed autistic students and their families to learn more about how they find the educational system and support systems in Ireland. The results were shocking:

• **35% said that they had to apply to four to seven different schools before they found a place for their child.**

• **54% said that the biggest problem was not having enough school places for autistic students, and 18% said that there were no suitable schools or classes near them.**

• **80% of those who were looking for a school place talked to their local SENO (Special Educational Needs Officer), but only 20% of those whose child was expelled or excluded did so.**

• **Some kids went to school full-time, some part-time, and some not at all. 17% of families said that their** child had a reduced timetable, and 13% said that their child had been out of school for up to three years!

- 54% of those families whose child(ren) were experiencing exclusion or extended absences from school were secondary school-aged, compared to 41% at the primary level.

- 91% of respondents whose child(re) were experiencing exclusion or extended absence from school said they were presently receiving no support from Tusla, the Child and Family Agency responsible for improving wellbeing and outcomes for children in Ireland.

- 66% reported that anxiety was the main reason why their child(ren) was experiencing exclusion or an extended absence from school, followed by 52% who believed that a lack of knowledge and understanding of autism was their main reason, as well as 34% who cited inadequate supports currently available in schools.

This shocked me. How can we expect autistic kids to learn and grow if they don't have access to education and support? How can we expect them to be happy and healthy if they don't feel accepted and valued? How can we expect them to thrive if they don't have a

chance? These findings highlight the need for more awareness and support for these children and their families. This report illustrates the main difficulties that students with Autism encounter in the education system, with a lack of understanding and acceptance from their peers and teachers. Students with Autism may have different learning styles, preferences, and needs than their neurotypical classmates, which can lead to social isolation, bullying, and discrimination. Moreover, teachers may not have adequate training or resources to support students with Autism in the classroom, resulting in low expectations, inappropriate curriculum, and ineffective teaching methods. These factors can negatively affect the academic performance, motivation, and self-esteem of students with Autism.

It's time for me to get on with my personal experience in the Irish education system. Starting with my primary school days as I have very little recollection of preschool but from the stories my mom told me, I would get bored easily with the same songs and games, I would just start daydreaming, asking to go home or just going to sleep instead of taking part.

Primary School

My days in primary school play like a scene from a home movie, it plays in my head and then stops mid-scene. I do not have any bad memories of my primary school days. However, at this stage of the book, it may not come as a huge surprise to you the reader to learn that I was not the popular girl in school. I did find great joy and comfort in books and the wonderful worlds I created in my head. I did spend a lot of time in my head during this time, maybe too much, I would even be excited to get to those times of the day I could get a chance to go back to these worlds. I loved to learn in school, but there are some aspects of schooling I struggled with, at the beginning it was predominantly socially related. I did not think it was such a big deal, I was much happier and more comfortable doing my own thing. However, when I was talking to my mom recently about my primary school days, I noted how I did not recall my lack of socialising skills. My mum on the other hand told me differently, I had not realised my teacher had noticed my mutism during school period and my lack of interaction with others and suggested to my

parents that I should be assessed. I don't know what kind of assessment she had in mind, but it never took place. Instead, I was sent to a special class once or twice a week where I could read more stories. I enjoyed that very much. I wonder what the purpose of that class was. Maybe they wanted to see if I had any learning difficulties or something… if anyone knows please contact I'm so curious. I wish I could remember the names of the books I read there. They had that distinctive smell, and paper feel, and the characters still linger in my memory. I feel they will be with me for the rest of my life, but I have no recollection of their name. I do remember, however, how much I hated getting called on by the teacher to answer a question, to read the next part of a paragraph or to read my homework out loud, these were nightmares to me. Speaking of homework, this is where I showed "bad" behaviour, and where for the first time in my life, I lied. It was not the homework itself I had trouble with it was the tension.

Thinking back now, maybe I was procrastinating to start, I did not read questions correctly, get confused and stressed very easily resulting in brain fog. The result tended to be lots of tears. To avoid this, I thought it would be easier if I just didn't have any homework. So, I told my parents I didn't have any, and skipped it. My

parents believed me, why wouldn't they, they had no reason to think I was lying. It was when I was called into the principal it all came out, and the shame. I will never forget that.

Another issue I tended to struggle with, then and to some extent today, is how difficult I can find transitioning between tasks when I'm not ready. I hated transitions or being hurried in any way this would result in extreme stress. For example, if the teacher erased the blackboard before I finished copying everything down, I would become so upset that I would even pull at my hair, break pencils, dig fingernails into my arms and face at times and cry. I know teachers who told me to calm down or students noticed and would inform the teacher, I was told I need to learn to get over it or write faster. I wish I had a way of recording the class. This was an issue throughout my school years, and I only learned to cope better when I went to university, thanks to the online lecture notes on a platform ironically called Blackboard. But there was one lecturer who used acetate slides instead, and sometimes he would take them away before I could write everything down. That same feeling of frustration came back. But I didn't let it get too far, and I just asked him to see the slide I missed after the lecture.

Ending primary school on a more positive note, I did eventually make some friends in primary school. Three lovely girls: Amy, Caoimhe and Mary. They were kind and just lovely people. I kept in touch with Caoimhe for a few years after I moved away and started secondary school, writing letters to each other which I thought was cool.

I will always be grateful to these three, especially when they stuck with me when the other girls in our class tried to exclude me. All the girls in the class went to Stillorgan, a suburban area of Dublin, and the majority of the other girls planned to leave me behind. But Amy, Caoimhe, and Mary didn't go along with their scheme.

They stayed with me, and we had a great day. The other girls are just a blur to me now.

Secondary School #1

In my opinion, this secondary school felt a lot more alienating than my primary school, maybe it's that transition into being a teenager, social life and friends become so important. I had some great teachers... And some terrible ones. My grades were all over the place. And I felt very uneasy around the other girls in my school. The only person I was close with and felt comfortable with was my cousin, who was always very nice, we were close and had spent summers and

Christmases together all our lives. She is a wonderful and caring person who made me feel welcome and accepted, which is probably why she would become a primary school teacher (I'm sorry, I tend to go off on tangents... A lot... And this might be one of the few books I write where that's okay, and hopefully expected)

... When she wasn't there, I would either wander around the school grounds, if the weather was good. Or I would roam the school corridors or hide in the bathroom. I dreaded lunchtime. To make things worse, some students liked to start fires in the stalls next to me or burn things outside my door. A teacher once commented on how often it happened as if to suggest I was the one doing it.

I did not quite understand why I could not socialise with the girls in this school, I did not know how to have a conversation. I did try sometimes. During these attempts, some girls (not all, some were lovely) would just look at me and look away. I do recall eye contact was extremely difficult at this time. Not only was it physically impossible to look into someone's eyes at this time, but maintaining eye contact when I had to was torturous, I would go red and be close to tears and be unable to speak. I do not look back at this time with particularly positive feelings. It was a very confusing time, even thinking back on it now I feel incredibly uncomfortable, and that confused feeling comes back. I had no idea what was expected of me and what was the right or wrong way to behave. What were the rules? Everything I did seemed to be the wrong thing. Then my mother would give me the greatest gift.

Secondary School #2

The Institute of Education was a life-changing gift, I do not think my mum fully knows the extent of just how much it gave me. Some people may have issues with private schools, but this place was somewhere I felt welcomed. I had the freedom to choose my subjects and create our schedule, we could even choose which teachers we wanted to be with, and we were given two weeks to try the classes out before we had to decide. I was treated like an adult, and it was expected we were there to work. The subjects were fascinating and engaging. If you were not there to work, you were gone. I liked that as I was easily overwhelmed and agitated by too much movement and talking.

My grades were good in a lot of my classes… not all, but I still struggled with exams. I did well on assignments, though. The teachers liked me (except for the chemistry teacher, but I dropped that subject anyway). Some of the teachers were very surprised that I did not do as well as they thought in my leaving certificate. As my continuous assessments had a strong consistent grade. Now I understand why: big halls, a lot of people, and a lot of noise. Too much going on. The only time this did not occur was during aptitude tests. Maybe it's because they were different, you didn't have to study, so there was no pressure, it was multiple choice and the time felt limitless. It was fun, it felt like a game or a puzzle.

Especially the spatial awareness section, which involved spotting patterns within shapes and involved manoeuvring the shapes in your head and visualising potential results. For example, you have a flattened "Box", below this is a selection of cubes, you must find the correct cube which would match the flattened box. For example:

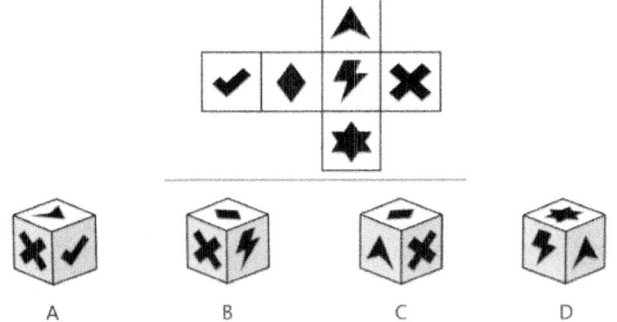

I recall doing this more than once, but I didn't mind, it was fun. A few days after I was brought to the guidance councillor's office with my mother. I was told I was within the top 5% in the country for spatial awareness (not sure what that means) and told I would suit a career as a dentist, or an architect… I just wanted to be a marine biologist, I told them this then we left and that was that. Very odd. I'm proud of it, but I have no idea what it meant and didn't assist in my career.

University- bachelor's degree

In university, I faced the same struggles as before: exams. This was incredibly frustrating as I was studying, I would step into the library at 8 and look up from my work when the library closed, and it was dark outside. Time was an illusion during those times. Little good that did during the exams, and I just could not understand why. No matter how hard I studied, I would find it very difficult to recall information. My brain was very foggy… another way I would describe it as like trying to grab hold of a river flowing by, you may grasp for a second then it would trickle away. I just could not take hold of the information I needed, it was incredibly frustrating and caused a lot of stress and anxiety during exams. I now know this problem with memory recall is due to poor Executive Function, which is the ability to plan, organize, prioritize, and focus on tasks and it also affects working memory. Without good working memory, it is hard to remember facts and figures that are essential for exams. These effects could get so bad they could result in panic attacks, these panic attacks.

The fourth year brought a new-found struggle in the writing of my thesis, I was ok at essays, but the thesis was another beast entirely. I tended to get distracted in the middle of a sentence, starting a new sentence without finishing the prior one. This resulted in sentences that just stopped, without punctuation or full stop, into a completely different, unconnected topic. Even worse I found it very difficult to read back, my eyes would feel like they were covered in a shadow and the words would be a blur on the page it was like scrolling quickly through a Word document and seeing nothing but a blur as you scrolled. I felt like people were understanding all these complex things and I was just not able to grasp it at all, this feeling was strongest during the writing of the thesis. I was constantly wondering what I was not getting. I did end up graduating with my bachelor's, just about.

My dad and I went to talk to my supervisor after I got my results to understand what went wrong. She was not particularly helpful, and we left more confused and frustrated. As we both knew I worked hard but missed something. One thing she did say that annoyed us was "It's like this, Laura would make a great surgeon and save the patient's life, but they would die due to the paperwork" ......????.   WHAT??? Although I really shouldn't be surprised, when I was doing my thesis, she never answered any emails I sent her any requests to proofread were never answered I also sent her an email about doing statistics never replied.... Now I'm thinking... should your final year supervisor be giving you more advice? Is that why I was so lost?

amazing, music to my ears, and it meant more to learn. Research is constantly evolving and expanding, and how exciting a concept is that. I felt like I was breathing pure oxygen, it felt amazing, and everything felt bright and clear. I was less stressed and more confident than I'd ever been. It was like seeing the world with new eyes. The only exam I did have to take was required to continue into my master's project, the minimum requirement you had to achieve was 55%. And I managed to pass it with 67%. If your mark was less than 55% you graduate with a higher diploma. I enjoyed the exam and felt focused. It was not a perfect score, but I was pleased and felt like an accomplishment.

My master's degree was a rewarding experience that boosted my confidence and skills. I excelled in my coursework and group research projects, even presentations. Once again, however, I struggled with writing a coherent thesis. Once again, I would often lose focus and wander off on tangents, leaving my sentences unfinished and my punctuation missing. This problem became more evident and more of a problem when I started my PhD, which required more rigorous and sustained writing. I will go into further detail in the next section.

I did struggle to maintain regular communication with my family during this time. I was so immersed in my studies that I often missed their phone calls or forgot to reply to their messages. I didn't do it on purpose, of course, but I was so fixated on my course that I would put it off. I always planned to call them back later, but then I would push it off again, and then I'd feel guilty and anxious about not talking to them for so long. This would create a mental barrier that made it harder for me to reach out to them. It was like a vicious cycle that kept me isolated from my loved ones. My mum recently brought this up and reminded me just how much they missed me and worried about me during this time.

University- PhD.

This is my current situation: I have no exams to worry about and I should be happy, but I had been getting increasingly depressed and anxious. I would be going between disassociating from my emotional state, feeling nothing, to getting overwhelmed. My self-esteem and confidence were obliterated, and I was consumed by self-doubt, not trusting any of my decisions.

I started my PhD with enthusiasm and passion, I had kept hold of my motivation, but it was faint, and my confidence was lost. It may not have helped that I took a full-time job that drained my energy and time. I worked from morning to night, every day of the week, without taking breaks or resting. I would be sick regularly, one resulting in a two-week illness and many sick days. I did have my wonderful son during my second year which resulted in more time off. Then nearly exactly a year later I had an emergency surgery due to an ectopic pregnancy. This could be a reason for the extensive stress as it was a bit of an upheaval and trauma, and I was just getting gradually worse.

I couldn't stop wondering what made me successful in my master's degree and what I was missing now. But then I realized that thesis writing was an ongoing trend. Once again thesis writing continued to be my nemesis. My supervisors could be confused and not understand what I'm trying to say or what my research question is. Executive Function once again. When executive function is impaired, it becomes difficult to write long and complex texts. That's why I'm putting a lot of effort into this book and paying attention to punctuation, coherence, and relevance.

I'm narrowing down my thesis topic and defining the main research question and objectives. I'm making a detailed outline of each chapter and section, with bullet points of what to include and exclude. And keep checking this. I am setting realistic goals and deadlines for each step of writing and editing. I am exploring various tools and techniques to assist me with writing, such as software, apps, books, podcasts, and blogs. Hopefully these all work.

That all being said there is one component that I am only recently connecting with success in writing and failure. Mood and emotional state, my PhD struggles were only really coming to the front in my third year, funny how you forget all of this when you are not in a good head space. Until my third year I was thriving, all my experiments were complete, my supervisors seemed happy, and they seemed at least almost as excited about the results as I was. I had interesting questions and hypotheses. I was happy with my teaching, and I was even a co-supervisor for a final-year bachelor's student. Then while writing chapter 2 of my thesis, I did the worst thing, since lying in primary school. I plagiarised, it was unintentional of course, I had never plagiarised before. I highlight the sections I take from papers, so I know to go back, read, interpret, and write in my own words, I had always been so careful, but I got distracted and removed the highlighted areas. For the life of me, I have no idea why. After the rebuking from my supervisors, I felt so much guilt and shame, I could not shake it and that was the start of the downward spiral. I could not let it go. And I could vocalise this feeling to anyone. The thing is my supervisors are nice people, and I know if I was able to talk to them, they would be incredibly understanding.

I've got to say this has been an eye-opening chapter for me. I had a bit of an epiphany and theory which I will utilise in the future. As writing a big project can be challenging for anyone, but especially for people with ADHD I will add some of the techniques:

- Break down the project into smaller tasks. Instead of trying to write everything at once, divide the project into manageable chunks, such as brainstorming, outlining, drafting, revising, and editing. Set a deadline for each task and reward yourself when you complete it.

- Use tools and strategies to help you stay focused. Some examples are setting a timer for each writing session, using noise-cancelling headphones or background music, turning off notifications and distractions on your devices, writing in a quiet and comfortable place, and taking breaks every 15 minutes or so.

- Seek feedback and support from others. Writing can be a lonely and frustrating activity, especially if you have ADHD. It can help to have someone who can give you constructive feedback, encouragement, and accountability. You can ask a friend, a family member, a tutor, or a professional editor to review your work and offer suggestions for improvement.

- Be kind and realistic with yourself. Writing a big project is not easy, and it may take longer than you expect. Don't beat yourself up if you make mistakes or encounter difficulties. Remember that you are not alone you have strengths and skills that can help you overcome the challenges. Celebrate your progress and achievements along the way. I am learning that your brain is sometimes just unable to work, and it may feel near impossible to concentrate, follow what your brain wants to do and eventually you will get there. This was a game changer for me and helped reduce stress, as fighting through it can add to your stress.

Chapter 6
The Workplace

I have worked in many workplaces, and positions, and been around an array of coworkers and managers throughout my career. From pet shops to an insurance company and five research facilities. Six out of three of these places had been extremely positive experiences, not a bad ratio.

In this chapter, I want to share some of my experiences with these backdrops and the managers that came with them. I will first talk about two of the most amazing places I worked then on to one that was not great. This one was so bad it had an extremely negative effect on my mental health. A few months before I was diagnosed with ADHD and autism, I hit rock bottom because of this toxic workplace. I will get into that later. First, I want to highlight the strengths that people with ADHD and Autism can bring to the workplace.

According to the ADHD Ireland website, some of the benefits ADHDers can bring to the workplace are:

- o The ability to hyperfocus on things they are interested in.
- o Willingness to take risks.

o Spontaneous and flexible

o Good in a crisis

o Creative idea – thinking outside the box

o Being motivated by short-term deadlines – working in sprints, rather than marathons

o Having a good eye for detail

People with autism likewise face a stigma and a high unemployment rate, but employers and society both gain from hiring workers on the spectrum. A new report published by the e-recruitment platform IrishJobs.ie and the autism charity AsIAm states that people with autism have valuable skills such as:

o Attention to detail.
o Analytical thinking
o Reliability and loyalty.
o Honesty and integrity.
o Creativity
o Systemising= Specialised interests and expertise

This report goes further into the challenges and opportunities for autistic people in Ireland. According to the report, 80% of autistic people are unemployed or underemployed and face barriers to getting the job they want. The report also shows that employers lack awareness and understanding of autism and need more support and information to create autism-friendly workplaces.

Several studies have shown that autistic professionals can be more productive than typical employees when properly matched to jobs. For example, Hendricks (2010) found that autistic employees had higher performance ratings than their non-autistic peers in a

software company. Hurlbutt and Chalmers (2004) reported that autistic adults who worked in fields that matched their interests and abilities were more satisfied and successful than those who did not. Müller et al. (2003) suggested that autistic workers had unique skills and strengths that could benefit employers, such as attention to detail, accuracy, and creativity. Therefore, it is important to recognise the potential of autistic people and provide them with reasonable accommodations and support to help them succeed in the workplace. By doing so, employers can not only improve the lives of autistic people but also benefit from their unique talents and perspectives.

Before I jump into my story, I want to share one of the

biggest things I learned from this journey. If I compare my weaknesses to somebody else's strengths, I will always feel down. Inevitably I will have strengths whereas others will have weaknesses and that's the way it should be. We will help each other. Some of the strengths I brought throughout my career were creativity, I found more efficient ways to do a job to make it more streamlined and get it done faster. I love to learn something new, when I was working in The Francis Crick one of the people who trained me said she liked it when she had to train me as I bring a lot of positivity. Another strength is how I handle chaos. I take it surprisingly well (now this is chaos in the form of hectic and we have to sort it out… not emotional chaos I go into later). When there was a lot of work to do, I am efficient, organised, clear-minded and productive. Short-staffed? No problem, I got it.

My weaknesses appeared when things slowed down, when this happened it was like my brain shut down. I couldn't think clearly or do anything sufficiently. Reading tedious documents could be so torturous, that I would be unable to see the words in front of me.

Something I faced in every workplace was social anxiety. I often found it hard to interact with my colleagues and managers when I first joined a new team. This has led to some negative feedback from my supervisors in the past, who expect me to be more vocal and engaged. I do eventually come out of my shell and build rapport with others. It just takes me some time to feel comfortable and confident in a new environment. Even then, new people or phone calls can be extremely stressful.

Now it's time to discuss two positive work experiences:

Job number 1: Carna research station was a wonderful place to work. It was in a remote area, so far away that my mom used to joke "Next stop USA". The work was fascinating and involved implementing welfare standards for fish, fish husbandry, taking part in physiological studies, and water quality testing. My colleagues were lovely, and there was only one enforced rule, which was to be on time. I know I know an ADHDers nightmare. But being on time was due to the needs of the animals, they needed feeding, cleaning and welfare checks were necessary. That was a good incentive for me to go in. The work was also really enjoyable, it looked at stress in cod and feed for salmon. While they are both well-known fish, generally as a food item, you may not know how much personality these animals have. Salmon are right wagons; they would jump at the slightest shadow, and they appear to be making a full-on attempt to get as much water out of the tank when you come too close. Cod, on the other hand, are like puppies. They stuck their heads out of the water, and follow you around from their tank, waiting for you to feed them. They were adorable. It was here I gained my interest in understanding the effects of stress on the health and welfare of marine animals. I also learned that stress could influence the immune system of the fish and that some genes are involved in the coping mechanisms. I was fascinated by how complex and diverse the stress responses are in fish. This would be what inspired me to do my master's and PhD in a similar area but in crustaceans rather than fish.

The manager of the station, Richard, was a very good person and a great friend. He was a fair and kind manager; Random input but he never rushed our lunch. Especially when the day was nice, and the main, important tasks were done earlier in the day. On those fine days, we could go snorkelling. When I talked to him about it, he laughed and said, "There's nothing else to do here, where else will you go", and he was right in the sense there was nothing but a church and a little hotel nearby. But we all wanted to be there to work too. We kept in touch after I left the station, and he gave me great advice after I got my bachelor's results. I was so low and lost, I thought I had ruined every opportunity to reach my dream of being a Marine Biologist. Unfortunately, he passed away in December 2016, I lived in London at this time and found out during one of our emails. In the last email he sent to me, he told me he had a chest infection, which was on 04/11/2016. He passed away on 5/12/2016. I still can't believe he is gone.

Job number 2: was in London, the Francis Crick Institute, was a big contrast to Carna, for it was based in London, one of the biggest cities in the world, a completely different world to Carna. I love London, it is my favourite city. My ADHD brain is in constant stimulation because it offers me opportunities to learn new things, meet different people, and explore a vibrant culture. I will not lie; migraines were the most intense when I lived in London. This was probably due to how stimulating the city was. The science, museums, architecture, and universities. Loved it all.

The institute was very prestigious and well-equipped, and I felt proud to be part of it, the research was also very interesting and learning about the work was fascinating. It was also more rigid for breaks, and lunchtime and you had to arrive at work between 7-9:30 which I liked. It suits me to have times I know are for breaks and lunch, it makes it much easier to create my routine. Each day of the week was on a routine but with a different main task each day.

I did make mistakes when we moved to the new facility, I was missing the birth of some pups as I forgot where I was in my checks. I was not the only one looking after the area my manager took me aside and enquired what could be done, as it was not like me to make mistakes (I hadn't considered why I was the one questioned, the other person sharing the work does get away with a lot more than he should). Either way, I requested notebooks. You see, notebooks have always been my secret weapon, they help me focus my thoughts, reduce mistakes, and provide comfort. They give me control. The notebooks arrived a few days later.

However, not everything was perfect at the Crick. There were some issues with the management and the culture that I did not agree with. I will not go into details, as they are not relevant to this book. I will just say that I do not support nepotism or bullying in any workplace, especially not in a prestigious research institute ... That's all I will say about that.

I have worked in jobs where I was either bored or unhappy, such as Costa and Petmania. They were not suitable for me, either due to the weird tension or not agreeing with the running of the establishment. I had worked in a small pet shop before, where the atmosphere was warm and friendly, and I believe they looked after the animals very well and at a much higher standard than the bigger chain pet shop. Sadly, it was outcompeted by this big chain store. Which was cold and unwelcoming. The bigger shop did not make animals the priority, it was all about the sale. I do not feel confident that the staff had any animal care experience. Health checks did not appear to be a priority. Very concerning. Especially when a guinea pig was having a seizure and they just brushed it off.

Now it's time to discuss the negative one:

Job number 3. My most recent place of work was a complete nightmare. I will not reveal the name, or any people involved, for my protection more than theirs. I would not put it past them not to sue for slander, even though this is all true. It was a terrible experience that I want to forget. Writing this part was surprisingly very hard for me. I don't know why, but it feels like this memory is blocked and when I try to remember it, everything is fuzzy and mixed up. I'm guessing it is due to the sheer negativity and confusion produced there, and still so confused and unsettled about that time. What I know for sure is that place was not good for anyone who values their sanity, and this is not a joke (If anyone wants to know where this place is, they can contact me privately, and I will also check with current employees if things have changed). People would quit all the time, and the only ones who stayed were either stuck there for too long or felt too old to change.

What didn't help my emotional state and could be the basis of most of my confusion was emotional mirror-touch synaesthesia. The Emotional component of mirror-touch synaesthesia means I feel what other people feel. This is not very convenient in a place where all of the employees are incredibly stressed. And when everyone was in one place, such as during a meeting, it got intense. These meetings could get so tense there would be an inevitable release, and people would just be yelling at each other. It was shocking.

In addition, these meetings should be an hour, but they would carry on for much longer. What was accomplished in these meetings? In between the tension and the yelling. Nothing. Just a lot of arguing and stress, that was it. The meetings did nothing for the work. Add on meetings being an ADHDers nightmare, I can usually keep myself engaged by writing, but that only worked for so long. The overwhelming negative emotions and the boredom would result in a two-day migraine, lasting from Friday to Sunday.

Laura G. A.

Now to the manager, the catalyst. She was highly
unpredictable in her managing behaviour, she would be
very criticising one moment, nothing you did was right,
then next you're great and she commends you. She made
me feel like I could never do anything right or have any
autonomy. She admitted in front of HR that she did not
trust her employees, which explained her treatment of
us, but it was still incredibly shocking to hear, even HR
couldn't hide their shock. Three of the employees had
been working for that institute for at least 12 years, so
they had been there before she was manager. In addition,
no one had ever done anything that would make her
doubt us. I suppose this explained her behaviour; it was
social whiplash. This resulted in more self-doubt, I knew
logically I had experience, and I never had these issues
in any of my previous places of employment.

We were expected to follow her instructions without
questioning them, even when they contradicted our
expertise or best practices. I must add, all of the staff
were highly trained and educated, for example, I had a
master's in animal behaviour and welfare; doing a PhD
in stress and anxiety behavioural responses, 5 years of
experience in preclinical and animal behaviour research,
and held an HPRA personal licence with the addition of
being a principal investigator in animal research

studies... My colleagues: PhD in chemistry; a
Veterinary degree and PhD; a medical doctor, and one
colleague who is probably one of the longest going
employees in that place, extremely knowledgeable. But
if we suggested new ideas or solutions, she dismissed
them without explanation. We had frequent meetings
that seemed pointless, since nothing we said was ever
considered. Once, a consultant was hired to improve the
work environment, he agreed with the manager that we
should just obey her orders. I disagreed and argued that
we should be able to voice our concerns and opinions,
as we were highly trained professionals who deserved
respect and trust. Yes, as manager she gets the final say,
but we are not in a dictatorship and that mindset will
create a sinking ship... it already had. I do think I made
her uncomfortable though, she may not like that even
though I can be shy and appear to lack confidence at
times, I will stand up for myself when someone was
trying to take advantage of me. For example, I taught a
biology lab once a week in the college I was completing
my PhD. There was an "agreement" that I would work
every weekend to make up for the time lost teaching.
The problem was I returned to continue work after my
teaching was over. We were moving to a new building,
so there was a lot of work to do, especially due to

everything moving to the new building having to be autoclaved. That is a lot of work and time, there was a volunteer who helped us pack and transport our equipment and samples. He was taking time away from his work to help us out, he didn't need to, but it helped a lot. So, I returned after teaching to assist. I thought this was a nice gesture, my manager knew, but she appreciated it at the time, not so much later. In addition, as my husband coached the university basketball team until 8, I would also stay and work during that time, then get a lift home. She knew this and once again, was fine at the time. Not so much when teaching finished and I told her I will go back to normal weekends, she didn't listen, she told me to organise with her second in command as he does weekends. Perfect I didn't go to work that weekend... No one went in that Saturday. She was furious and blamed me. Nope not my fault, that was her and her second to organise thank you. She called me into her office and tried to intimidate me into continuing the weekends, as I had more time to make up for teaching.... Ummm nope, I'm glad I keep very good time keeping records. I had already accumulated 52 hours of overtime, and that was not counting the weekends I deserved double the time. I refused to comply with her unreasonable demands and showed her my sign-in sheet as proof of my work hours. She tried to silence treatment me, just staring at me with this intense glare. But I did not back down, I was in the right, if I am wrong, I will always admit, apologise, and fix it. I would not be so adamant about this I was certain; I like to keep track of timings and organise numbers. So, there's a long-winded example.

The job itself was not stimulating enough to counteract the stress and horrendous treatment. The days when things got hectic could be exciting and a nice distraction. Due to the stress created by that work environment, after 3 years, I was making more mistakes, and the more mistakes I made, or perceived I made would cause me to feel anxiety and fear, and I was disgusted with myself. This resulted in me going down a negativity spiral, it was becoming a dangerous cycle, I knew I was nearing my breaking point, but was in complete denial. I was always angry, overly emotional, and then disassociating, becoming completely unfeeling. Calling in sick too regularly, while I can count on less than two hands my sick days in the past. I was having regular meltdowns; I was not a nice person to live with. Looking back, I did not make the number of mistakes I thought. I now know I was getting very close to burnout.

Burnout is a state of physical, emotional, and mental exhaustion caused by chronic stress. It can lead to symptoms such as fatigue, insomnia, depression, cynicism, detachment, and reduced performance.

My final manager story will maybe give you more of an idea of what she was like as a person not just a manager. I had some incredible colleagues. One, in particular, was a beautiful, kind, and gentle person…. the last meeting with this manager was odd and uncomfortable. She was bringing up the colleague I considered a friend, accusing this colleague of causing stress in the unit and being a negative presence… She was not the problem, not the one causing the stress. It got weirder when she informed me, she wanted to be my friend but couldn't as it would be inappropriate due to her position.

I do feel that this working environment was an outlier, as I'd never been in a place like that before. But I added it as a cautionary tale, it was not normal and should not be seen as normal. I want to see a change in working environments, and I believe it would not just benefit those who are diagnosed with ADHD and/or Autism, but everyone.

I will veer away from my stories and look at how the working environment can be improved. Once you get a diagnosis one of the most important decisions you can make is whether or not to disclose your diagnosis to your employer. This is a personal choice that depends on many factors, such as the type of job, the culture of the workplace, and your comfort level. Some of the benefits of disclosing your diagnosis are getting more understanding and acceptance from others, reducing the stress of hiding or masking, accessing workplace accommodations that can help you perform better, and raising awareness about neurodivergence among your

co-workers. Some of the drawbacks of disclosing your diagnosis are facing stigma and discrimination, being treated differently or unfairly, and having your abilities or qualifications questioned. There is no right or wrong answer to this question, but you should weigh the pros and cons carefully before deciding.

Just going to add that according to the Employment Equality Acts 1998-2015, it is illegal in Ireland to discriminate in the workplace due to a disability. This means that employers cannot treat employees or job applicants less favourably because of their disability unless there is a genuine and reasonable occupational requirement for doing so. Employers also have to provide reasonable accommodation for employees or prospective employees with disabilities unless this would cause undue hardship to the employer.

Reasonable accommodation means making appropriate changes or adjustments to the workplace, work practices, equipment, or facilities to enable a person with a disability to perform their duties effectively. Examples of reasonable accommodation include modifying work hours, providing assistive technology, allowing flexible leave arrangements, or offering alternative work assignments. Some people are afraid that disclosing their diagnosis to a potential employer might cost them a job opportunity (even though this is illegal, some employers can find ways to avoid hiring them). I wonder if I would want to work in such an environment anyway.

To get workplace accommodations, you usually need to disclose your diagnosis to HR and provide documentation from your doctor. This is often necessary to request and receive the support you need. Clear communication with your manager about your needs to do your work and fulfil your duties is most important. If you are concerned about privacy, you should know that many accommodations — like having agendas and notes for meetings — can be done discreetly. However, if you don't disclose your diagnosis to HR formally, your boss can legally refuse your informal requests for accommodations.

Different types of accommodations can help neurodivergent employees work better, communicate better, and feel better in the workplace. The best accommodation is the one that suits you. For example, having uninterrupted time for work is also essential. Many employees with autism or ADHD say that it's hard to resume work after being interrupted, whether by a coworker asking a question or by a manager asking for help with something that's not urgent. To prevent losing your concentration and getting distracted from a task, you might want to set up Do Not Disturb hours. What helped me at The Francis Crick Institute is having the radio playing, it helped with routine and keeping me focused I listened to Radio X, and I knew the rough time due to who the host was. For example, when The Chris Moyles show was over it was break time. According to ADDitude workplace advocacy comes in many forms, including the following:

- Education: Learning about invisible disabilities and how they affect work performance and relationships.

- Flexibility: Accommodating different needs and preferences of employees with invisible disabilities, such as schedules, deadlines, or communication styles.

- Transparency: Being open and honest about one's well-being and encouraging others to do the same.

- Allyship: Supporting and standing up for employees with invisible disabilities and challenging stereotypes or misconceptions about them.

- Access: Providing easy and confidential ways for employees to request and receive tools, resources, or modifications that they need to work effectively and comfortably.

- Belonging: Creating a sense of inclusion and appreciation for all employees, by celebrating diversity, fostering collaboration, and providing feedback.

- Feedback: Encouraging open communication and dialogue among all employees and soliciting feedback on how to improve the workplace policies and practices to support them.

Workplace advocacy benefits not only employees with invisible disabilities but also the whole organisation. It can improve employee engagement, productivity, creativity, loyalty, retention, and satisfaction. It can also enhance the reputation, brand image, customer service, and social responsibility of the organisation.

My preferred work style is to have clear and specific guidance on what I need to do and how I will be evaluated. I appreciate having written instructions, visual aids, and checklists to help me stay on track and avoid mistakes. I can adapt to change, but I expect to be informed of any changes that affect my work in a timely and consistent manner. I don't like it when there is confusion or miscommunication because someone was left out of the loop. I also value a consistent and professional relationship with my manager. I recognise my manager's role and authority, but I also expect them to recognise my autonomy and competence. I don't need them to befriend me or micromanage me. I am driven and dedicated to doing a good job, and I believe most of my coworkers are too, everyone I've worked with wanted to be there was positive and worked to their best ability.

Chapter 7
Relationships

This chapter will explore the different relationships you may experience in life. These include familial, friendships, and romantic relationships. Relationships are essential for human well-being; even if we deny the influence of our relationships on our personality, they can affect us in positive and negative ways. We can learn from our relationships and discover what we want and need from others... Or maybe, most importantly, what we don't need. What I mean by this is that some people may prefer to have fewer or no relationships at all.

Maybe they would prefer friendships with their animals, and that's ok too. Those you have relationships with don't have to be human.

A message to parents and their relationships with their autistic child: receiving an autism diagnosis for your child can be a stressful and emotional event. As a parent (or guardian), you may want to learn more about your child's condition and how to support them.

You have the best knowledge of your child, but you may still have questions about how to help them with challenges such as:

- sensory overload
- a strong interest in topics or activities
- difficulties with communication
- preventing or managing meltdowns.

  Various strategies can be used to help your child, such as modifying their environment and surroundings, adapting how you communicate with them, and preparing them for change.

Get to know what causes overstimulation and teach your child to recognise the feelings they get and help them find something to calm it. A smell, music, headphones, heat, cold, holding something, stroking something. Let them have controlled times with their interest daily, this helps me. If I don't get access to my interest, I will get stressed, I will not be able to stop thinking about it or concentrate on anything else until I can access my special interest.

I will begin with the first relationship we all have the *familial relationship*. You could say future relationships are based on those you form in early life. I may not be strong with the rules of social norms, but my family did teach me that I deserve to be treated with respect, and never take bullying from anyone. I do believe I have come this far because of my family, by forcing me to step out of my comfort zone, and by finding courses that would allow me to thrive, such as the Institute of Education and my master's course.

I do face one challenge with my close family: masking. Masking is when I hide my true self and act like someone else to fit in. I have stopped masking with my husband and son, and with strangers and friends, but I still mask with some family members. The uncertainty of something I say could be hurtful, inappropriate, or come out the wrong way/ taken the wrong way, I screen everything I say. This is hard for me; I have made some progress, and I am more comfortable, but I still hold back from being fully authentic. If they say something that I interpret as a harsh criticism of my character, I will obsess over it. I could become so overwhelmed by this that I would dread visits and become more nervous in case I would do something wrong. If I received criticisms about how I dress or how I communicate (Too much or too little) I would feel like I was disappointing them or failing them somehow. Even though I know it's irrational, of course, it is, sure they can say they like this or that, but it's an opinion, not that they love or like me less. So yes, I know it is irrational, and I understand that now. With that extra sensitivity that I have to rejection and emotional dysregulation, there is that fear that the relationship with close family can suffer.

I do think covid and the isolation it brought, not to mention a new baby at the same time made this worse. The fact I was starting to feel that way with my dad, I was becoming more awkward in his presence. That was odd, expecting him to judge something I said or my appearance when he had never done it before. I am not sure why I would have thought he might suddenly start. Thankfully, this ended when we had an hour-long conversation about dog breeds over coffee.

My life has changed for the better since my diagnosis. I understand myself more and I feel more confident and relaxed. My mum has told me she has noticed a difference, and my parents are extremely supportive. I still have some challenges with communication and social situations, but they are not always as overwhelming as before. Baby steps.

I have a large and loving family that includes aunts, uncles, cousins, and a grandmother. I grew up with them, I have the fondest memories of spending summers, Christmases, and holidays together. I consider my cousins' siblings, they are the aunts and uncles to my son, not first cousins once removed. When we are spending time together, I can just be myself, and I love that. Yes, covid did create a separation that living in London did not create. Four of my cousins are primary school teachers, just-born teachers, and no doubt those kids love them. I would like to see them more often, but we have busy lives and different responsibilities. And not driving, I do need to get on with it and get my licence.

Friendships are complicated, and everyone's comfort level and definitions of friendships differ. Supposedly, the 'norm' for the number of friends a person should have been 5-8. However, you may be more comfortable in your own company, which was the case when I was younger. I was very content having little to no friends, I never mind leaving friendships behind. Or maybe you're comfortable with 1 or 2 close friends, or your partner and kids are enough. To some people their pets are their friends, I know I was one of these, and will be again when can have pets again. My pets were two rats called Pooka and Cooper, they made me very happy. Adored their company and I would be so excited to get home from work to see them. If you go looking for more friends, just make sure you ask yourself: do YOU want more friends or if this is to appear normal for others' sake? Do you have the emotional capacity and energy for additional friendships? Now I appreciate my friendships more and realise I need to spend more time with them, but I also need to get a better understanding of my capacity and limitations.

I love the friends I have! They are all amazing and special and bring so much in their ways. And they understand me, and I understand them. They are also the kind of people who don't always reply to messages, so they don't get mad when I don't either... But sometimes I wonder if they are my friends or just people I know. I don't make or keep friends in the usual way. If I meet someone who likes the same things as I do (like at a conference), we can talk for hours about our passions, and I feel like we are best friends. It's so fun and thrilling. But I heard that a good friendship takes 6 months to a year to develop, to build trust and intimacy. I tend to skip that part and just chat about my interests, without thinking if it's too personal. This is great when our interests align. This can make me vulnerable later, especially if I didn't set boundaries or notice red flags.

This has happened to me before when I trusted people who did not treat me the way anyone should be treated. I tended to make more friends with boys than men growing up. This was not a problem in childhood, but more of a problem in adulthood. I liked male friendships because they usually talk more about their hobbies and activities or do things together. That suited me. Girls and women tend to be more emotional, which is okay when it's just two of us but not so much in a group. Saying that since taking this journey, something incredible happened, I found this amazing ADHDer community on Instagram. And now a few of us have formed a What'sApp group. It is still early days, but such a good idea and I have never felt like I belonged somewhere so much.

In general, I do tend to struggle with social communication, I also get easily overstimulated and exhausted by too much social interaction, especially if there is a sudden appearance of new individuals I was not prepared for. Concurrently, I crave the stimulation of being around other people and engaging in social situations. I struggle not to overbook myself socially because invitations sound fun and exciting at the moment. Plus, I have a hard time saying "no" because as a late-diagnosed neurodivergent adult I've developed people-pleasing tendencies. This is common in those who have had a lifetime of trying to not upset people or be rejected. When the arrival of a social outing has arrived, I usually feel fear and dread, once in a social situation, my ADHD means I find myself talking too much, struggling to not interrupt people or oversharing. This, for my socially anxious autistic side, is intolerable, not so much in the moment as it happens. When I get home, however, I overanalyse everything I've done and said, and feel anxious about further rejection. And EXHAUSTED. This is precisely the case after my son's third birthday, 4 days ago, I have been exhausted, emotionally drained and quick to frustration the last few days. I am slowly coming back to myself.

One of the challenges that I face in my relationships with others is my difficulty in communicating effectively.

Sometimes I avoid answering the phone or replying to texts because I'm afraid of what the other person might say or ask me or worse how I would reply. I get anxious about the possible topics or moods that could come up. This is something that I'm trying to overcome by forcing myself to answer the phone and be more responsive. I know it's not good to ignore or delay communication with my loved ones. If I put it off, it will get undeniably worse and mix guilt into the anxiety it becomes a downward spiral.

Another issue that I have is that I tend to misunderstand or be misunderstood by others. I think I'm being clear about my intentions and actions, but occasionally the other person doesn't get it. Maybe I didn't mention it enough times, or maybe I only said it in my head and not out loud. This can cause confusion and frustration for both of us. I also have a habit of oversharing information that I find interesting or useful, without paying attention to the other person's feelings or interest level. I love to learn and share facts and logic, but sometimes I don't notice when the other person is bored or annoyed by my rambling. They might tell me to shut up or walk away, and then I feel hurt and confused. I had wondered if I was a bad person or a psychopath for not being more empathetic.

However, not all communication is hard for me. My husband is great at understanding me and engaging with me in stimulating conversations. He likes to come up with theories and hypotheses, and he now knows that when I say, "I don't know, what about a, b, c or d" I'm not dismissing him but inviting him to a debate. We have fun and exciting discussions where we explore different perspectives and possibilities. I don't mind being wrong or corrected, as long as I learn something new. If someone shows me evidence that contradicts my view, I'm happy to follow it and change my mind. If I am wrong and find out after the person has left, however, I will stress about that as I need to tell them this, I'd even get awkward and have to inform them of my mistake, even if it is weeks later.

Romantic relationships. I had considered this before, but

after some research, I will finally admit I am asexual.

Asexual people do not experience sexual attraction, which means they do not feel the desire to have sexual intercourse with others. I have never been interested in sexual relationships, or any romantic relationships. I never showed any interest in them, I preferred platonic friendships and I'm incredibly uncomfortable with anything more. I tried to be normal here, but I don't like it and even now typing about it I feel odd, a bit uncomfortable.

I also never had romantic crushes on movie characters or celebrities. I get friendship crushes if that's a thing. I imagined them as my friends, real people were hard work, while pretend were so much easier.

I had my first kiss in secondary school because I was being called a "fridget". I didn't know what that was, but it didn't sound like a good thing. Just made me feel like more of an outsider. I did not have my first "proper" relationship until I was 21, 3rd year of university. I wouldn't even call it a real relationship but was my closest. I started a relationship because I got the impression I needed to be in a relationship, while I would rather not have been. My relationship status came up regularly in conversations when I was home.

Eventually, I just thought FINE, someone said they liked me, so I went with it. This was not fair on the person as I had no idea what a relationship was, I just went through the motions of what was expected of me. I was in Galway and the guy was 1.5 hours away, so we only saw each other once a month, that was ok with me, but that wasn't a real relationship. I also did not feel comfortable with the times we were together. So, when I did brake it off, it was the right thing to do. Although it was not clean, and supposedly I was not clear in my communication of this.

This is why meeting the man who eventually become my husband was such a surprise. I was not kidding about not being interested in sexual relationships I didn't even feel comfortable being in the same bed as someone else, did not like skin touching me. I never thought I would get married and if I did, I was certain we would have to sleep in separate beds. That changed when I met my now husband.

On our first date, I did not know it was a date at the time, we held hands, and I liked it! I don't do handholding, as you know touching was not something I was a fan of.

We connected on a deep level, and he respected my boundaries. He did not pressure me to do anything I was not comfortable with. He made me feel safe. When we did have our first kiss, he asked for my permission, very much the definition of a gentleman.

I felt it was very important to bring up the topic of grief, and processing grief and how that can impact neurodivergent individuals. I put this in relationships as grief usually stems from a loss in a relationship, namely death. Autism and grief are two complex and challenging experiences that can affect people in different ways. People with autism may process and express their grief differently from neurotypical people and may need differences in support and understanding. For example, some people with autism may have difficulty identifying and naming their emotions or may show them in unusual ways, such as laughing, rocking, or repeating words. Some people with autism may have strong attachments to routines, objects, or places, and may struggle to adjust to the absence of a loved one.

Some people with autism may have sensory sensitivities and may find certain aspects of funerals or memorials overwhelming or distressing. Some common myths about autism and grief are that people with autism do not feel emotions, do not understand death, or do not need to grieve. These myths are harmful and untrue and can prevent people with autism from getting the help they need. People with autism feel a range of emotions, including sadness, anger, confusion, fear, and loneliness. They can also understand death at different levels. They may need more time, repetition, and concrete explanations to grasp the concept of death and its implications. They may also need more guidance and structure to cope with the changes and losses that death brings. People with autism have the right to grieve in their way, and to be respected and supported by others. Similarly, people with ADHD may experience grief differently than others, and they may face some unique challenges when coping with loss. Some of these challenges include:

- Difficulty processing emotions and expressing them appropriately.

- Trouble staying focused and organised during stressful times.

- Increased impulsivity and risk-taking behaviours

- Feeling overwhelmed by the demands of daily life

- Feeling isolated or misunderstood by others.

This was more than true for me after my grandmother died, it was a confusing time. I was not coherent, and I was not organised. I got muddled with times and was not a good communicator to my husband about the funeral and the lead-up.

If you have ADHD and you are grieving, some of the

strategies that may help you are:

- Seek professional help from a therapist or counsellor who understands ADHD and grief:

- Join a support group for people with ADHD or for people who have experienced a similar loss.

- Practice self-care by getting enough sleep, eating well, exercising, and doing activities that bring you joy.

- Set realistic goals and prioritise your tasks.

- Use reminders, calendars, timers, and other tools to help you stay on track.

- Reach out to your friends and family for emotional support and practical assistance.

- Be gentle with yourself and acknowledge your feelings without judging them.

I had to add the death of an animal companion, when an animal dies, I feel this so powerfully. I have less control over my emotions and actions. I do get a negative reaction from others, who do not understand why I act in such a way, especially when they were "just" _insert animal type_. Losing an animal companion can be extremely painful for anyone, especially for autistic people who can have a strong bond with their pets. Animals can provide unconditional love, comfort, and support to autistic people, and losing them can cause intense grief and sadness. Here are some ways to cope with grief after the death of an animal companion:

- Acknowledge your feelings and express them in healthy ways. You may feel angry, guilty, lonely, or depressed after your pet dies. These are normal reactions, and you have the right to feel them. You can talk to someone you trust, write in a journal, draw, or do any other activity that helps you process your emotions.

- Remember your pet and honour their memory. You can keep some mementoes of your pet, such as their collar, toy, or blanket. You can also make a scrapbook, a photo album, or a video of your pet. You can visit their grave or place a marker in your yard or garden. You can also donate to an animal shelter or charity in their name.

- Seek support from others who understand. You may feel isolated or misunderstood by others who do not share your grief. You can look for support groups, online forums, or websites that are dedicated to grieving pet owners. You can also reach out to friends or family members who have lost pets or who are empathetic to your situation.

- Take care of yourself and your needs. Grieving can take a toll on your physical and mental health. You may lose your appetite, have trouble sleeping, or feel anxious or depressed. It is important to take care of yourself by eating well, getting enough rest, exercising, and seeking professional help if needed.

- Be patient and gentle with yourself. Grieving is a process that takes time and varies from person to person. There is no right or wrong way to grieve, and no set timeline for healing. You may have good days and bad days, and that is okay. Do not compare yourself to others or judge yourself for how you feel. Remember that you are not alone and that you will get through this.

I am going to acknowledge this chapter is quite heavy and we are not going to get any lighter…This next paragraph will be discussing trauma and sexual assault. I intentionally put it at the end of this chapter, so you have the choice to skip it entirely if you do not want to read it. I will start with trauma and end with sexual assault (This will be put into italics).

Trauma is a common and diverse experience that affects people in different ways. For neurodivergent individuals, who have differences in brain structure and function, trauma can be especially challenging and pervasive.

Neurodivergent people may face more stress and trauma due to social stigma, discrimination, misunderstanding, and lack of support. They may also have difficulties with emotional regulation, sensory processing, and cognitive processing that make coping with trauma harder.

we experience something that overwhelms our

to cope, our brain may not be able to process it
properly. Normally, our brain processes our memories
during sleep, especially during REM sleep, and transfers
them to long-term memory storage. During this process,
the memories are emotionally and cognitively integrated,
so they lose their emotional charge and become part of
our narrative. However, when something is too
traumatic, this process fails, and the memories remain
stuck in our short-term memory. These memories can be
triggered by anything that reminds us of the traumatic
event, such as sights, sounds, smells, places, or people.
When this happens, we may feel intense emotions of
fear, anger, sadness, or guilt. We may also develop
negative beliefs about ourselves or the world that are not
based on logic or reality. Our amygdala, the part of our
brain that is responsible for detecting threats and
emotions, becomes overactive and puts us in a state of
trauma. When trauma is not processed, we cannot make
sense of what had happened, if someone is
neurodivergent yet undiagnosed, they can find it very
difficult to understand and process traumatic experiences
that might have occurred. Negative experiences in
school, friendships or the workplace have particular
effects for those who are neurodivergent, due to not

having the information and knowledge to understand why that happened to them and that it is not their fault. We are all doing the best we could.

Traumatic experiences are sometimes categorised into Big T and Little t traumas, the main difference between Big T and Little t Trauma is the event that catalysed the traumatic response. Big T trauma is related to life-threatening events, such as a natural disaster, a violent crime, a car accident, or a shooting. This would also include acute psychological traumas such as the death of a family member. Chronic trauma such as repeated abuse can also qualify as big T trauma.

Little t trauma refers to events that typically don't involve violence or disaster but do create significant distress. Rejections from a social group, bullying, exclusion, negative comments, criticised for something you can't help, criticised for something other family members are capable of. Repeated exposures can produce the same trauma responses as big T Traumas. Some experts contend that this distinction between Big T and little t is problematic and potentially harmful. They argue that what may seem like a little t trauma to one person may be a Big T trauma to another, and vice versa. They also warn that labelling some traumas as big or little may imply a value judgment or a hierarchy of suffering, which may invalidate or minimize the experiences and feelings of some trauma survivors. They advocate for a more holistic and individualized approach to trauma assessment and treatment, that considers the person's context, history, and needs.

This is extremely valid, ultimately, any event or ongoing situation that causes distress, fear, and a sense of helplessness qualifies as trauma. And trauma can have serious mental, physical, and emotional impacts on young people, negatively influencing daily functioning and relationships. Traumatic stress is associated with a higher risk of suicide, as well as anxiety, depression, and co-occurring issues, including substance abuse, and eating disorders.

Trauma can affect us in many ways, both physically and mentally. Our body and brain have a natural defence system that helps us cope with dangerous situations.

This system is often called the "fight or flight" response or the "fight, flight, or freeze" response. But sometimes, this system can also have other reactions that are less helpful or adaptive. These are known as fright, flag, and faint. Here's what each of these responses means:

Fight: When we choose to confront the threat, our heart and breathing rate increase, giving us more energy and strength.

Flight: When we decide to escape from the threat, our muscles get ready to run away if needed.

Freeze: When we face a threat, our brain scans the environment to assess the level of danger. Our senses become sharper to gather more information.

Fright: When we feel overwhelmed by the threat, our fear takes over and makes it hard to think rationally.
Flag: When we feel hopeless or helpless, our body starts to shut down and we feel numb or detached.

Faint: When we experience extreme trauma, our body sometimes responds by losing consciousness.

These responses might make sense when we are in a life-threatening situation, such as a fire, a car crash, or a violent attack. However, sometimes our nervous system can't tell the difference between a real danger and an emotional one. That's why small traumas can have the same impact as big traumas. And sometimes, our nervous system can keep reacting even when the threat is gone. This happens because our brain and body haven't processed and released the trauma yet.

For Autistic people, many small traumas that happen every day can add up and cause Complex Post Traumatic Stress Disorder (C-PTSD), while a sudden big trauma can cause Post Traumatic Stress Disorder (PTSD).

This leads me to sexual assault, so a trigger warning was issued until the next chapter:

Sexual assault is a horrific crime that affects millions of women around the world. But did you know that neurodivergent women, such as those with autism or ADHD, are even more vulnerable to this violence? A recent study published in 2022 by Cazalis and colleagues showed that there is a higher percentage of assault in neurodivergent women than in neurotypical women. Their research indicates that about 30% (1 in 4 in some studies) of women in the general population have been sexually assaulted, but this rises between two to three times as much for autistic women. That means that 9 out of 10 autistic women have been sexually assaulted! And 2/3 of the assaults occurred before the age of 18.

Female ADHDers have a 2x increased risk of sexual assault. These are staggering and heartbreaking statistics that demand our attention and action.

Why are neurodivergent women more likely to be sexually assaulted? There are many possible factors, such as social isolation, difficulty with communication and consent, lack of awareness and education, stigma and discrimination, and increased exposure to abusive situations. Neurodivergent women may also face barriers to reporting and seeking help after an assault, such as not being believed, being retraumatized, or not finding appropriate services. In the study by Cazalis and colleagues, only 25% of the 113 women who reported an assault got the help they needed and followed through, while 75% had no action or assistance. This is unacceptable and unjust.

Sexual assault can have devastating consequences for neurodivergent women's physical and mental health. It can lead to brain damage, depression, anxiety, insomnia, PTSD, substance abuse, self-harm, and suicide. It can also affect their sense of identity, self-esteem, trust, relationships, and sexuality. Neurodivergent women (as does everyone) deserve to live in a world where they are safe, respected, and supported. They deserve to heal from their trauma and thrive in their lives.

We need to raise awareness and prevent sexual assault against women as a whole. We need to educate ourselves and others about neurodiversity and consent, to challenge the stereotypes and myths that dehumanize and objectify neurodivergent women. By doing this we can create safe spaces and communities where neurodivergent women can connect and share their experiences, providing accessible and trauma-informed services and resources for neurodivergent survivors are highly required. By doing this we are not only improving the world for neurodiverse women but all women. Everyone can benefit from this mindset.

It has been found that there are no specific risk factors relating to autism and ADHD traits and sexual assault, predators are very good at choosing those who are vulnerable. They pick a person due to ease, separating a person from others. Feeling different, you tend to have internal feelings of separation from others. You cannot trust your own decisions; can't trust your feelings and you can't trust how you interpret the situation. Been told all your life you are wrong; some people can take advantage of this vulnerability. For myself, I thought the person who assaulted me was my friend, and as such I acted the same way as I would with my female friends, there was no difference in my eyes, which may be what blinded me. I was even dropped there by my now husband (we were not going out at the time, just good friends). I had stayed in this person's house before on the sofa, this time I stayed in their bed after a lot of too and froing on who would take the sofa and bed. I was so tired by that stage I just wanted to go to bed. I was woken up by a weird sensation between my legs, my pyjamas had been pulled down and his head was already there. I froze, I was confused, I don't know what he was doing, and I didn't understand why. I told him to stop, and he did, and he left. I did not go back to sleep, I did not leave, I did not move, I disassociated. I do not remember anything about the next day or going home.

My first memory following that is his message which stated that he was glad I was so cool about it as girls tend to not be. Those words have stuck with me all these years. I had suppressed that memory and had no intentions to return to it until Ashling Murphy was attacked and murdered and the uproar that followed. I started to talk about it, I burst into tears and told my husband. After that I was calm when I brought it up again to two friends and my therapist, I thought I was fine. And I was fine for a while, it wasn't until a scene in Alice in Borderland (over a year after my admission) and the severity of my reaction that I realised there was more to it. During a scene a disgusting individual was assaulting one of the main characters, he stared to lick her inner thigh and my fingers started to go numb, I got nauseous and the next thing I knew I was gasping for air and in tears. It happened so fast. I was so angry with myself for the reaction, which made me realise I was still more angry at myself than the individual. I have to still remind myself that even though I was in his bed I did not consent. I was asleep and he was supposed to be on the sofa, that may be rude of me, but he was supposed to be on the sofa. I still have a lot to work on, I don't know how to approach the subject with my therapist, at least to talk about it in the way I need to rather than changing the subject when I do bring it up.

I will end this chapter here, I will add that it does not say anything about you or your values as a person, your intelligence, or your assertiveness, it's about the person who carried out the act.

Chapter 8
Home is where the Heart is!

There was an internal debate concerning where to place this chapter, and whether to include it with my relationships chapter. In this chapter, I decided to focus on what home means to me. This choice was due to my home being my safe place. As home is where I feel safest, however, this means it is also the place where most, if not all, of my meltdowns occur. Home is where the mask should naturally fall off, where anything and everything you hide from the outside world is unleashed. When it comes to school-age children it can be normal for them to mask at school and have a complete meltdown when home. This is due to them hiding who they were all day and being physically and emotionally exhausted. So, to parents facing this, your child has masked to exhaustion and now they feel safe enough to take the mask off. My advice here is to let you and your child have a sensory reprieve. For the child who is overwhelmed by excessive noise, try offering them ear defenders, and calming earbuds (or headphones) and let them sit in silence or allow them to use an MP3 player to control their environment.

For sensitivity to light, let them sit in calmer lights try

using a desk lamp instead of overhead lighting or my favourite lava lamp or fairy lights. If they are sensitive to smells, maybe there is a mild scent or essential oil that could be diffused and allow them to sit in that. I carry peppermint and chamomile with me everywhere, if I feel overwhelmed, I smell one.

These meltdowns were the biggest problem I brought home after work. Before I even considered getting a diagnosis, I started therapy due to my meltdowns becoming so frequent (they were daily). I would come home from work and feel like a mess. I had to pretend to be normal and put up with so many negative emotions all day long, which was exhausting and frustrating.

Overly stimulated and overwhelmed, from hiding my true self all day and just downright confused by the behaviours of others, especially my manager. Who was the most confusing person, could not give clear instructions, would take no ideas, and would shut down any opinions. And would go from buttering you up to making you feel awful in one day, for no reason.

When home I was so exhausted and confused, I would go from one extreme to the next, from excited, and happy to angry in seconds. Without any warning, I would just snap at my poor husband. Who's just minding his own business, oblivious to the ticking time bomb beside him. The smallest things could trigger me: loud noises, too much movement, or the smell of overcooked broccoli. I would lose it; I would yell and cry completely unable to handle the overload of sensations. I was like a toddler having a meltdown, with no control over my emotions. This was not good for me or my family. It created a lot of tension and stress. It didn't last long, but it left me feeling guilty, ashamed, and tired, and my husband feeling hurt and frustrated. And the worst part was, my son could be within earshot.

I didn't want that for him. I didn't want him to be afraid of me or to worry about when I would snap next. I knew I needed help. I went to therapy and learned that I had poor emotional awareness. I didn't know what I was feeling or why. I didn't know how to cope with my emotions or express them in healthy ways. My therapist gave me some exercises to practice every day. I had to sit down for five minutes and pay attention to what I was feeling and what was happening in my body. Was it a good or a bad feeling? What caused it? And then I had to say to myself, "This is what (insert emotion here) feels like". It helped a bit, I started to notice some changes.

But I still had some blind spots. Sometimes I would still go from calm to furious in seconds, without any warning on. It took me a while (until I got diagnosed) to ,stand why.

It was after my diagnosis I became aware of Alexithymia, hypersensitivities to noise and smells, and emotional dysregulation as the factors that can cause my emotional state to go from 0-100 within seconds. With the diagnosis of a condition that makes me more prone to these episodes, I have learnt some coping strategies that help me calm down and prevent these meltdowns. For example, right now I can sense that I am getting overwhelmed as I write this. So, what do I do? I try to expose myself to sunlight, which has a soothing effect on me. If the weather is cloudy, I use a hot water bottle instead. I wear comfortable clothing, like an oversized jumper or a robe. I turn on my diffuser and inhale the relaxing aroma of chamomile and peppermint. And I engage in passive work, such as typing notes or extracting information from research papers. These actions help me lower my stress level and regain control.

I am still feeling a bit edgy, but much better than before. I remind myself to drink more water and take care of myself.

With a chapter titled Home, I have to bring up the elephant in the room, this is a chapter about home…and

what inevitably coincides with home: housework. (Cue
the horror movie soundtrack of choice). Housework is
the nemesis of most people with ADHD, and it can also
be a source of self-conflict for those with a dual
diagnosis of Autism. On one hand, you crave order and
stability in your environment. On the other hand, you
feel overwhelmed and paralyzed by the sheer number of
tasks that need to be done. And so, you procrastinate and
procrastinate, and procrastinate some more. I used to
beat myself up for my inability to complete this task,
especially when I compared myself to my relatives who
had spotless homes. But that's ok, my husband and son
are very supportive and understanding of me, and they
don't nag me or judge me for not cleaning up right away.
They love me for who I am, not for how tidy I am. So, I
learned to be kinder to myself and to accept that my
house will not always look like a magazine cover. And
that's okay. It's my home and my sanctuary. It's where I
can be me, and where I feel safe and happy. That's what
matters most. Make your home work for you, not against
you. I'm lucky to have two amazing guys who let me be
me. My son is incredible, an incredibly outgoing and
friendly little guy, unlike me. If I did not have him in my
life, I would not know anyone in my estate. I regularly
go for coffee in 2 houses and feel a part of the

community, it's a cool feeling.

If you want tips on making housework more manageable and fun for people with ADHD, check out How to ADHD- ADHD Friendly House Hacks on YouTube. It's a great video that will make you laugh, smile, and learn something new.

Chapter 9
ADHD, Autism and Healthcare

This is such an important topic I had to designate a chapter purely to physical health, and the experience those with ADHD and/or Autism have with the medical care system. Neurodivergent individuals may face various physical health challenges that are related to their neurological differences. For example, those who are neurodiverse are more likely to experience pain due to hypermobility, which is a condition where the joints are more flexible than normal. Hypermobility can affect more than 50% of neurodivergent people, compared to 20% of the general population. There is also the tendency to have gastrointestinal (GI) problems, dysautonomia (such as dizziness on standing up), or increased sensitivity to sensory stimuli. These physical health issues can affect the quality of life and well-being of neurodivergent people and may require medical evaluation and treatment. However, neurodivergent individuals may also face barriers to accessing health care, such as stigma, discrimination, or lack of understanding from health providers.

Children with Autism have an almost eight times higher risk of having one or more chronic GI symptoms compared to children without Autism (Chaidez et al., 2014). Recognizing GI symptoms in people with ASD can be especially challenging, as some individuals are non-verbal and many have impaired communication, making it harder for them to express pain or discomfort (Buie et al., 2010). GI symptoms can also worsen ASD symptoms, such as behavioural problems and social difficulties, and lower the quality of life of individuals with ASD and their families (Madra et al., 2020).

Therefore, clinicians need to understand how these GI issues present and apply effective therapies. Treating GI problems in ASD may result in significant improvements in ASD behavioural outcomes.

Interoceptive issues could probably be self-protection mechanisms. This is very likely my case, as a young child I would have a lot of stomach pain, my mum informed me the pain would at times result in seizures. This could be where my interoceptive issues stem from. There are studies that back this, Goodall, 2022, for example, suggested that GI pain may reduce or stop the development of interoception skills. For example, they may avoid paying attention to their internal signals because they are too overwhelming or painful.

Interoceptive issues can affect various aspects of medical

health, such as:

- Chronic pain: People with interoceptive issues may have trouble identifying the source, intensity, or quality of their pain, or may have distorted perceptions of pain due to emotional factors. This can lead to under- or over-treatment of pain, reduced quality of life, and increased psychological distress.

- Eating disorders: People with interoceptive issues may have impaired awareness of their hunger and satiety cues or may have negative associations with certain bodily sensations related to food intake. This can result in abnormal eating behaviours, such as bingeing, purging, restricting, or over-exercising.

- Cardiovascular diseases: People with interoceptive issues may have difficulty detecting changes in their heart rate or blood pressure or may have exaggerated responses to stress or anxiety. This can increase the risk of developing hypertension, arrhythmia, or coronary artery disease.

- Diabetes: People with interoceptive issues may have poor awareness of their blood glucose levels or may have difficulty managing their insulin injections or oral medications. This can lead to hyperglycemia or hypoglycemia, which can cause serious complications if left untreated.

The studies have found that adults with Autism do not show impaired interoceptive accuracy, suggesting that they may overcome or compensate for their early interoceptive challenges (Nicholson et al., 2019). For example, they may learn to use external cues or strategies to help them identify and regulate their internal states. Therefore, interoception is a complex and dynamic phenomenon that may vary across the lifespan and individuals with Autism.

This reduced perception of pain intensity resulted in many emergency surgeries in my life. When I was 14 or 15, I fell off my horse and flew into a barrel, I jumped back on and continued with my day. A few weeks later a huge black and blue bruise was forming around the area I had made an impact with the barrel, and my breasts were swelling and a bit uncomfortable, I also fainted in school. My mum was concerned especially when she saw the bruise, I was brought to the doctor. Who referred me to the hospital. An ultrasound later I was rushed to surgery due to internal bleeding resulting in sepsis.

This example is to provide awareness of the potential for doctors to not understand the full extent of an issue. I had an ectopic pregnancy two weeks after my son's birthday. I had some discomfort in the lower left side of my abdomen. While it was not painful, it was not normal. So, I mentioned it to my husband, and he flagged it as a concern and insisted we go to the out-of-hours doctor. The on-call doctor was incredible, he gave me a once over and said it may be kidney stones, but he highly recommended we head straight to the emergency room. We did. Not long after arrival, I was informed I was pregnant... I put two and two together and knew it was an ectopic immediately. But the nurses and doctors were not sure as I did not present as an ectopic. I stayed in the hospital from Monday to Thursday without getting the necessary scan. It was Thursday evening after two ultrasounds that it was confirmed I did indeed have an ectopic pregnancy in my fallopian tube and it had ruptured, I was bleeding into my abdomen... SO another rush into surgery.

This is not unusual for individuals with autism and interoceptive issues, a young girl whose appendix burst was not presenting as "normal" appendicitis, but a nurse noticed the stimming behaviour near the affected area and connected the dots.

Pregnancy can affect neurodiverse individuals in different ways that should be discussed. Pregnancy can be challenging for those with ADHD and Autism, as they may face various physical, emotional, and environmental difficulties. Some of the challenges that pregnant people with ADHD and Autism might experience are:

- Sensory differences: They may be more sensitive to sounds, light, taste, touch, personal space, and eye contact. Resulting in feelings of overwhelm or discomfort in certain situations, such as medical appointments, labour, or postnatal care.

- Communication differences: They may prefer clear, unambiguous language, or broken-down information. They may also have trouble expressing their needs, feelings, or preferences to others. This can affect their understanding of the pregnancy process, their decision-making, and their relationship with their care providers and partners.

- Anxiety: They may be very anxious in an unfamiliar environment, or not knowing what to expect over an appointment, pregnancy, or parenthood. If things become too stressful, they may experience a 'shutdown' or a 'meltdown', which can be exhausting and require time and space to recover. Some may cope by avoiding treatment and care, which can lead to health inequalities and risks.

Some of the best practices are:

- Structure: Having a predictable routine and environment can help them feel calm, safe, and in control. This can include having continuity of the same care team throughout, clear guidelines and processes to help manage expectations, opportunities to meet staff and visit the ward before labour, and a personalized care plan that reflects their needs and preferences.

- Positivity: Being positive, kind, and understanding, without bias or judgment. Being supportive of their decisions and taking their lead. Providing encouragement and praise for their achievements and coping skills.

- Empathy: Being empathic when communicating and trying to reduce anxiety and distress. Using questions such as 'What do you need to feel ok?' Also, being accepting of self-soothing behaviours and accommodating of their sensory and communication preferences.

- Information: Providing clear, concise, and accurate information about the pregnancy process, the possible risks and benefits of different options, and the expected outcomes. Using visual aids, written materials, or other formats that suit their learning style. Allowing them time to process the information and ask questions.

- Involvement: Involving them in the decision-making process as much as possible. Respecting their autonomy and consent. Seeking feedback from them about their satisfaction and comfort level with the care provided.

I felt it was necessary to share my childbirth story as a

neurodivergent person. I don't know if many doctors or nurses understand how there can be differences between those with ADHD and Autism. Sometimes we don't notice or feel exactly what is happening in our bodies. In addition, we may not always speak up about our discomfort or worries either due to fear of being annoyed or misunderstood or we don't know how to articulate how we are feeling or what is happening. As I discussed in the chapter on my childhood, I have interoceptive issues, which means I have trouble sensing what's going on inside me. I have a high pain tolerance and a low awareness of when something is wrong.

Childbirth was not very painful for me, but it was very confusing. I didn't need any painkillers, but I also didn't know when or how to push. I had to rely on the doctors to tell me what to do, but they didn't always understand me either. Sometimes I felt like I had to poop, and I asked them if I should push, but they said no.

The day after the birth I felt great, I was walking around and getting used to being a mom. In the afternoon, however, after what was supposed to be a quick trip to the bathroom while a midwife did some quick checks on my son. Did not quite go according to plan, my body just stopped, and I could not move, I only had enough strength to hit the bell for assistance. Midwives had to help me back to my room, I had never in my life felt this weak. When they checked my haemoglobin levels, they could not believe I had been walking around for so long, I had lost 3 litres of blood during the birth, and I had no idea anything had been wrong until my body just could not physically hold me up anymore.

I know it's not easy for doctors or other medical staff to try and decipher the needs of neurodivergent individuals, but tools to assist doctors in determining what is going on with their patients in an efficient fashion would be highly advantageous. Neurodivergent individuals often have difficulty communicating their needs and feelings to doctors and other medical staff, especially in stressful situations. This can lead to misunderstandings, misdiagnoses, and inadequate care. By being aware of these signals, doctors can better assess the condition and comfort of their patients and provide them with appropriate treatment and support. Some suggestions:

One possible tool that medical professionals can use to understand the body language and stimming behaviours of neurodivergent patients is a visual guide that shows different types of stims and what they mean. For example, rocking back and forth, flapping hands, or tapping fingers could indicate anxiety, excitement, or boredom. The guide could also explain how to respond to these stims in a respectful and supportive way, such as asking the patient if they need a break, offering them a sensory toy, or giving them space.

Another possible tool is a communication card that neurodivergent patients can use to express their needs and feelings without having to speak. The card could have icons or words that represent common requests or emotions, such as "I need water", "I'm in pain", "I'm scared", or "I'm happy". The patient could point to the card or hand it to the doctor to communicate their message. The card could also have a scale that shows the level of sensory overload or distress that the patient is experiencing, from low to high.

A third possible tool is a sensory kit that contains items that can help neurodivergent patients cope with sensory overload or stress. The kit could include earplugs, headphones, sunglasses, weighted blankets, fidget toys, or calming scents. The doctor could offer the kit to the patient and let them choose what they want to use. The kit could also have instructions on how to use the items safely and effectively.

Chapter 10
Diagnosis and Treatment

Wow, you made it this far into the book! That's amazing! I'm so happy that you stayed with me for this journey of self-discovery. I hope you gained something from it. You're almost at the end. Maybe you found some of my stories relatable, or maybe you learned something new about yourself or someone you love.

Either way, I hope this book was a positive and helpful experience for you. And if you are a parent of a child with ADHD or Autism or Both, I hope this book gave you some insight and reassurance that your child is not alone or broken. They just need some extra support and compassion.

I wanted this chapter to be a conclusion to my first chapter, before introducing you to the stories of other people living with ADHD and/or Autism.

When I wrote Chapter 1, I was waiting for my official diagnosis report. Well, today 29/05/23, I got it. And I now have an official diagnosis:

*"**Adult Attention Deficit Hyperactivity Disorder, combined presentation type.** The above-described difficulties are pervasive (across >2 settings) and long-*

standing (non-episodic). There is evidence of impairment in education, work, social life, free time, and self-confidence."

This report was like a validation of my whole life. It explained so many things that I struggled with and felt ashamed of. It showed me that there was nothing wrong with me, I just had a different way of thinking and behaving. It also made me feel that someone understood me, someone who was an expert in this field. I have this ongoing fear of being misunderstood, and this psychiatrist got it, everything in the report was how I felt and the parts of myself I felt shame for were described in a clinical way that gave me comfort. It was very direct and matter-of-fact, as if to say of course that is the way you are, and don't try to be any different.

Even my Mental State Examination (MSE) was a breath of fresh air.

"MSE

Alert, orientated, pleasant, forthcoming, good rapport, fluent, relevant, at times tangential, coherent, emotional – content appropriate, euthymic, nil psychotic, nil aggressive features, nil suicidal thoughts/intents/plans, discrete clinical signs of distractibility and evident psychomotoric ill-at-ease during the interview, presentation consistent with long-standing difficulties focusing and self-disorganisation as well as (inner)restlessness and difficulty relaxing, bright and driven endearing young woman."

Now that I have my diagnosis, I have started my treatment, the treatment options are designed to suit my needs and goals. For the time being, I am continuing my therapy, and I will continue with this as long as I can as it has helped me so much. One of the recommendations from my psychiatrist was coaching, which sounds like a good idea to me. I think it would help me with my PhD studies and my mental health in general. Maybe I'll give it a try someday soon.

I'm so happy to share with you that I have also started taking medication which personally has been a game changer. There is a lot of debate about medication for ADHD, but in the end, that decision is down to you. ADHD medication can be divided into two types: stimulants and non-stimulants. Stimulants are more commonly prescribed, and they work by increasing the levels of certain brain chemicals called Dopamine and Noradrenaline. Non-stimulants also affect these brain chemicals but in a different way. They may be used when stimulants are not effective or cause unwanted side effects.

In Ireland, there are two kinds of stimulants available: Methylphenidate and Lisdexamfetamine:

Methylphenidate is the most widely used stimulant for ADHD. It comes in different forms that vary in how long they last in the body:

- Immediate-release Methylphenidate (Medikinet IR or Ritalin IR) lasting about 4 hours and must be taken several times a day. For example, a person may take one dose in the morning before school or work, another dose at lunchtime, and a third dose in the afternoon.

- Modified (slow) release of Methylphenidate (Medikinet MR / Equasym XL / Concerta XL) lasts for 8 to 12 hours and can be taken once a day. For example, a person may take one dose in the morning and have a steady effect throughout the day.

- Lisdexamphetamine is another stimulant that works similarly to Methylphenidate. It is often considered when Methylphenidate does not work well or causes side effects. The brand name in Ireland is Tyvense. This medication lasts for about 10 hours and is taken once a day. For example, a person may take one dose in the morning and have a similar effect as the modified release Methylphenidate.

Non-stimulant medications are alternatives to stimulants. They include:

- Atomoxetine ("Strattera") is a non-stimulant that works by blocking the reabsorption of Noradrenaline in the brain. It has a 24-hour effect and can be taken once a day. For example, a person may take one dose in the evening and have an improved attention span the next day. It may be suitable for people who have ADHD and tics, or who cannot tolerate stimulants.

- Guanfacine ("Intuniv") is another non-stimulant that works by stimulating certain receptors in the brain that regulate attention and impulse control. It may also help reduce oppositional behaviour that is often seen in people with ADHD. For example, a person may take one dose in the morning and have fewer arguments or tantrums during the day.

- These medications are not addictive, and they do not make the person feel high. They help the person focus better, control their impulses, and manage their emotions. They may take some time to start working and they may have some side effects such as headache, nausea, loss of appetite, or sleep problems. These side effects usually go away after a few weeks of taking the medication. The person should follow the doctor's instructions on how to take the medication and report any concerns or changes to the doctor.

- I'm very happy to share my experience with Tyvense, a medication that has helped me a lot with my ADHD, I am currently on 20mg of Tyvense. I love that I don't feel like a different person on this medication, I still have my personality and my energy, but I have more control over my attention and my actions. I can switch between tasks more smoothly and I don't get overwhelmed by the mess in my house. I can deal with it at my own pace, and it doesn't affect my mood or my self-esteem.

- The biggest change that Tyvense has brought to my life is that I can focus better on what matters to me. I noticed the difference almost immediately. Only two hours after taking it. I could feel my head clearing, it was like a fog lifted from my mind and I could see things more clearly and calmly. I realized how chaotic and noisy my thoughts were before, and how much they were holding me back. Now it feels like my thoughts are lining up nicely, waiting for their turn to speak. And everything is more vivid and enjoyable. In addition, after the first day, I did not need energy drinks to help clear my head, I haven't touched a monster or Reign. Energy drinks are not great for me, once the effects wear off, feeling worse than before the drink. In addition, the tvyense effects are much smoother and I feel less chaotic and more present. I'm more organized in the mornings, my son is always ready to go to his daycare well before we have to leave. I'm having more fun with him instead of worrying about all the things I have to do. And I'm prouder of the work I've done by the end of the day.

- I was working on my thesis, and I was able to stay focused on the task I was doing even when I moved to the next page and was able to follow a sentence and spot errors. An option I have used is Lion's mane mushroom and ashwagandha coffee made by the Cheerful Buddha. Now I can only speak personally of their effects, I do feel like they help clear my head and help with my organisation and focus. I am more likely to clean up the house after a cup. So, it could be helping reduce the stress caused by the thought of cleaning and open me to it, who knows?

- I don't like promoting something without a basis so here's what I know about Lion's mane mushroom and ashwagandha. The Lion's mane mushroom and ashwagandha are two natural substances that have been used for centuries in traditional medicine for various health benefits. Some people claim that they can help with ADHD. But what does the scientific evidence say about these claims?

Lion's mane mushroom is a type of fungus that grows on trees and has a distinctive appearance resembling a lion's mane. It contains bioactive compounds such as polysaccharides, hericenones, and erinacines, which have been shown to have neuroprotective, anti-inflammatory, and antioxidant effects. Lion's mane mushroom may improve cognitive function by stimulating the production of nerve growth factors and repairing nerve cells. It may also reduce symptoms of anxiety and depression, which are common in people with ADHD.

Ashwagandha is an herb belonging to the nightshade family and has been used in Ayurvedic medicine for thousands of years. It is known as an adaptogen, which means it can help the body cope with stress and restore balance. Ashwagandha may improve cognitive function by enhancing memory, attention, and executive function. It may also reduce stress and anxiety, which can interfere with attention and concentration.

There is no conclusive evidence that lion's mane mushroom and ashwagandha can cure or treat ADHD. However, some studies suggest that they may have beneficial effects on cognitive health and mood, which could be helpful for people with ADHD. However, more research is needed to confirm their safety and efficacy for this condition. Before taking any supplements, it is advisable to consult with a doctor and follow the recommended dosage.

When it comes to Autism and treatment, first, I will have to say there is no cure for Autism. But various forms of treatment can help people with Autism function better and reduce their symptoms. Some of the common forms of treatment are:

Medication treatment: This is a type of treatment that involves using drugs to manage some of the symptoms of ASD, such as anxiety, depression, irritability, or hyperactivity. Medication treatment should be prescribed by a doctor and monitored regularly. Some of the common drugs are selective serotonin reuptake inhibitors (SSRIs), antipsychotics, stimulants, and anticonvulsants. For example, an SSRI may help a person with ASD reduce their anxiety or obsessive-compulsive behaviours. An antipsychotic may help control aggression or self-injury. A stimulant may help a person with ASD improve their attention span or impulsivity. An anticonvulsant may help prevent seizures or mood swings. Medication treatment can have side effects and interactions, so it is important to consult with a doctor before starting or changing any medication.

Behavioural management therapy: This is a type of therapy that has received increased levels of controversy in recent years, in particular Applied behavioural Therapy (ABA). I add ABA for educational purposes, as information has been going around and it is hard to grasp. However, according to Gruson- Wood (2016) Applied behavioural therapies are commonly used interventions that have become the standard of healthcare and expert knowledge for autistic people in Canada. These therapies are individualised methods of behavioural modification that teach skills and regulate socially "undesirable" or "inappropriate" behaviour according to expert claims (these terms used "undesirable" and "inappropriate" concern me) .

The methods focus on correction, imitation, repetition, reinforcement, and environmental modification. Despite their prevalence, these therapies are highly controversial within autism communities. While non-autistic parents and clinicians are their main proponents, autistic self-activists are their critics. There is a valid argument that it is harmful and unethical. They argue that behavioural management therapy is based on a deficit model of autism that pathologizes and stigmatises autistic traits and experiences. They also make a case that behavioural management therapy is coercive and abusive, as it forces people with ASD to conform to neurotypical norms and expectations, disregards their autonomy and consent, and causes psychological distress and trauma.

The promoters of this method claim it teaches people with ASD how to modify their behaviours and cope with challenging situations. Stating it can also help them to learn new skills and improve their social interactions. Behavioural management therapy can be delivered by trained professionals, parents, or teachers. For example, a therapist may use positive reinforcement to reward a child with ASD for following instructions or sharing toys. A parent may use visual cues or schedules to help a child with ASD understand what to expect and what to do next. A teacher may use structured activities or peer modelling to help a child with ASD participate in the classroom. Other approaches to behavioural management therapy can be based on pivotal response training (PRT), or discrete trial training (DTT). These approaches use different methods to teach and reinforce desired behaviours and skills.

There are several alternatives to Applied Behavioural Therapies (ABT) that can be used to help autistic individuals and could be safer and more appropriate. Here are some of them:

Cognitive Behavioural Therapy (CBT): This therapy focuses on identifying and changing negative thought patterns and behaviours. It can help individuals with autism learn to manage their emotions and improve their social skills. I have personally worked with my therapist using this form of therapy. I used it to help recognise my emotional state and raise awareness to how my body reacts during differing emotional states.

DIRFloortime Therapy: This therapy focuses on building relationships and communication skills through play-based activities. It can help individuals with autism develop their social and emotional skills.

Relationship Development Intervention (RDI): This therapy focuses on building relationships and communication skills through real-life experiences. It can help individuals with autism develop their social and emotional skills.

Music Therapy: This therapy uses music to help individuals with autism improve their social, emotional, and communication skills. It can help individuals with autism learn to express themselves more effectively.

Speech-language therapy: This is a type of therapy that helps people with ASD to improve their speech and language skills. It can also help them to understand and use nonverbal communication, such as gestures, eye contact, and facial expressions. Speech-language therapy can be provided by speech-language pathologists or other specialists. For example, a speech-language pathologist may use pictures or symbols to help a child with ASD learn new words or concepts. A specialist may use social stories or role-playing to help a child with ASD practice conversational skills or social etiquette. A speech-language pathologist may also use augmentative and alternative communication (AAC) devices or apps to help a child with ASD express their needs or wants.

Speech-language therapy can address different aspects of communication, such as articulation, fluency, voice, pragmatics, semantics, and syntax.

Occupational therapy: This is a type of therapy that helps people with ASD to develop the skills they need for daily living, such as dressing, eating, grooming, and using tools. It can also help them to adapt to different environments and sensory stimuli. For example, an occupational therapist may use sensory integration techniques to help a child with ASD cope with noises, lights, or textures. An occupational therapist may also use play-based activities or games to help a child improve their fine motor skills, such as holding a pencil or buttoning a shirt. An occupational therapist may also teach a child strategy to organise their belongings or manage their time. Occupational therapy can address different areas of functioning, such as sensory processing, motor skills, cognitive skills, self-care skills, and leisure skills.

Equine Assisted Therapy (EAT) involves interactions between humans and horses. EAT has been shown to have a positive effect on autistic individuals and other neurodivergent people, such as improving communication, social skills, emotional regulation, sensory processing, and motor skills. EAT can also provide a fun, engaging, and stress-free environment for learning and personal growth.

According to Liskennett Farm, a centre for children and adults with autism in Ireland, EAT incorporates the "Horse Boy" method, which is designed to enable autistic people to "meet, learn, play and express themselves" with the help of horses. ChildVision, another Irish organisation that provides EAT for children with sight loss, complex needs and neurodiversity states that EAT can also enhance academic skills such as maths, literacy, biology, and ecology. EAT can be delivered in different ways, depending on the needs and preferences of the individual. Some common forms of EAT are:

- Therapeutic riding: This involves learning how to ride a horse with the guidance of an instructor. Therapeutic riding can improve balance, coordination, posture, muscle strength, and confidence.

- Hippotherapy: This involves using the movement of the horse as a tool for physical, occupational, or speech therapy. Hippotherapy can improve sensory integration, body awareness, speech production, and cognitive functioning.

- Equine-facilitated learning: This involves engaging in educational or recreational activities with horses, such as grooming, feeding, or playing games. Equine-facilitated learning can improve problem-solving, decision-making, communication, and social skills.

- Equine-facilitated psychotherapy: This involves working with a mental health professional and a horse to address emotional or psychological issues. Equine-facilitated psychotherapy can improve self-esteem, empathy, trust, coping skills, and emotional regulation.

EAT is a promising and evidence-based intervention for autistic individuals and people with other neurodivergences. However, it is important to note that EAT is not a cure or a one-size-fits-all solution. EAT should be tailored to the individual's goals, needs, interests, and abilities. EAT should also be delivered by qualified professionals who have experience and training in working with horses and

neurodiverse populations. EAT should be part of a comprehensive and holistic treatment plan that includes other forms of support and therapy.

I visited an equine-assisted learning centre in Moate, co. Westmeath. Its objective is to improve our communication, trust, boundaries, stress management, self-awareness, personal development, and social skills. The lady behind this centre is Patricia Roarke, she had a natural intuition to connect and communicate with all clients verbal and non-verbal communicators. All personality types and activity levels. She has 3 golden rules when in the arena with the horses and ponies, to keep the animals and clients safe. I was there for just under an hour, yet my mental state and mood were extremely positive for a week, and I didn't even have a session. When I met Patricia, I had a few questions.

1) How did you get started in Equine Therapy?

I was giving a presentation on horses and grooming. After a stranger who works in mental health approached me and said I should train to do Equine Assisted

Learning. I had never heard of this before, not a clue what it was. But as soon as I got home that evening, I googled it, and I was hooked. While I was interested, I put my name on the waiting list, I used this time to get the money saved. However, I was not completely sure if I had made up my mind to do it. This changed when my friend died of cancer, before she died, she said I had to do the course and left me the money for it.

When I initially started the course, I was leading a stubborn little pony and thinking what the hell am I doing here? Dragging this pony who seems to want to be here as much as I do, that's where I had my Eureka moment. This pony was acting this way as it was reading it from me. As soon as I realised this my mindset changed and the stubborn pony was no longer stubborn.

2) Who do you take as clients, what are the age ranges and are you looking for more?

Equine Assisted Therapy is not just for children with special needs, I would like to work with anyone who feels they need it. I am trying to improve my methods of advertising. I would like to work with the parents of the children I work with, and I strongly believe it will help cancer survivors, abuse survivors and anyone who went through trauma.

For age groups it depends on the individual, supposedly under 12s are hard to work with as they cannot understand their emotions. A parent approached me one day and begged me to give their 4-year-old a chance. I agreed and it was a huge success. The child who was hyperactive and could not take directions was calm and helped me tidy up the arena when I asked. His mother was delighted. So, I now take 4, 5, 6,7-year-olds and up with serious results.

3) What does a session involve?

Each session depends on the individual. Younger children tend to have 20-to-30-minute sessions as that's all their attention span can allow. The sessions could be grooming the horses, mucking out, or emotional literacy or feeling. I use dressage letters A, K, E, H, C, M, B, and F and have the client attach a feeling to each letter and they can put it around the arena. They can lead their horse around and go over jumps or obstacles to get to the feeling they need or what they want. I Don't Know is also an appropriate feeling, we don't always know how we feel.

One young girl was contemplating suicide and assigned the letter K the word Kill (myself) and the letter C with Care, when she attempted to lead the horse to the letter

K, he refused to go anywhere near it, pulling her towards the other letters. This appeared to be an eye-opening moment for the girl.

4) You mentioned you travelled, what does that involve and what is necessary?

I will travel to schools or workplaces, anywhere that has a safe area to work, preferably away from the grass to not tempt the poor horses.

Other methods of treatment include:

- **Educational and school-based therapies**: These are services that schools provide to help students with ASD succeed in their academic and social goals. They may include special education, individualised education plans, classroom accommodations, and specialised teachers or aides.

- **Early intervention**: This is a term that refers to providing support and treatment for children with ASD and their families as early as possible, usually before the age of three. Early intervention can help children with ASD develop their skills and abilities and reduce the impact of their challenges.

- **Joint attention therapy**: This is a therapy that aims to improve the ability of people with ASD to share attention and interest with others, such as looking at the same object, pointing, or following someone's gaze.

Joint attention is important for social communication and learning.

- **Nutritional therapy**: This is a therapy that involves changing the diet or adding certain nutrients for people with ASD. The purpose of nutritional therapy is not to cure ASD, but to address some of the issues that people with ASD may face, such as:

1) Gut upset: Some people with ASD may have gastrointestinal (GI) problems, such as stomach pain, constipation, or diarrhoea. These problems can affect their mood, behaviour, and health. Some people with ASD may find that avoiding certain foods, such as dairy or gluten, or eating more fibre or probiotics can help their GI symptoms. A nutritionist or a doctor can help with this. I used to get abdominal pain daily, it was so normal to me it would be odd if I did not get stomach pain every day. It was only when I got older, I realised that was not normal. I have found reducing the consumption of certain dairy products and a slightly carb-free diet helped a lot with my abdominal pain. But everyone is different, Someone trained in this area can be a huge help.

2) Food hypersensitivity: Some people with ASD may

have allergic or intolerant reactions to certain foods, such as eggs, nuts, or soy. These reactions can cause symptoms such as rashes, hives, swelling, or breathing difficulties. These foods should be avoided and an allergist or a doctor should be consulted.

3) Eating a limited diet: Some people with ASD may prefer to eat only a few foods that have similar colours or tastes, such as white bread, cheese, or crackers. This can lead to nutritional deficiencies and health problems. A nutritionist or a doctor can help with expanding the diet and adding supplements if needed.

- **Physical therapy**: This is a therapy that helps people with ASD improve their physical skills, such as balance, coordination, strength, and endurance. Physical therapy can also help with sensory issues, such as being over- or under-sensitive to touch, sound, or movement. A physical therapist can design exercises and activities that are fun and suitable for each person's needs and abilities.

- **Parent-mediated therapy**: This is a therapy that involves training parents to deliver interventions for their children with ASD. Parents can learn how to use strategies such as praise, prompts, modelling, and reinforcement to help their children learn new skills and behaviours. Parent-mediated therapy can also help parents cope with stress and improve their relationship with their children.

Chapter 11
Let Me Introduce You To....

Jane's Story

For years, I navigated the challenges of school and college feeling completely misunderstood, seemingly falling short of expectations despite my obvious potential. I flew under the radar, with my school and college results wrongly attributed to a lack of trying. Little did others know that beneath the surface, I battled with undiagnosed ADHD, an invisible force hindering my ability to close the gap between average and completely acceptable grades to a higher standard that my parents and teachers knew was within my reach, yet none of us could understand why I just couldn't get there.

Despite being caught hanging from a ceiling beam by a teacher during lunch hour, nobody questioned my behaviour because I was generally quiet in class. Little did they know I was on another planet, daydreaming about anything more interesting than the room I was forced to sit in. The stereotypes surrounding ADHD can be exasperating, reducing it to a collection of disruptive traits rather than acknowledging its biological origins and impact on brain development and function. This is particularly true for women, who often experience hormonal imbalances that manifest as emotional dysregulation. The constant and overwhelming emotions I was feeling came to a head exactly 4 weeks after I had the contraceptive bar placed in my arm. I never noticed the timing, nor did my doctor who promptly issued a sick cert for 4 weeks off work, which sadly turned into 52 weeks (spoiler alert: I clicked back to myself exactly 4 weeks after having it removed).

Due to the additional hormones exasperating my symptoms, during this time I was unable to function like a normal 25-year-old woman. I endured a turbulent period of eight months on antidepressants, prescribed without a thorough investigation into my brain health, I began questioning the treatment I was receiving as I had no improvement. It became evident that my dark thoughts and self-perception were symptoms of an underlying brain-related issue. Despite repeatedly expressing my belief that something was amiss in my brain, medical professionals relied on guesswork rather than conducting necessary tests, akin to examining any other vital organ with scans and tests. Instead of providing me with tools to manage my emotions, the medication felt like a jack-in-the-box, with my feelings springing forth once the tablets were discontinued.

Harnessing my innate critical thinking and problem-solving skills, I conducted my research and decided to explore organic alternatives. Micro-dosing magic mushrooms emerged as a potential avenue. With nothing to lose but my sanity, which had already been hanging by a thread, I embarked on this unorthodox journey. Remarkably, within a mere two weeks, I experienced a profound shift in my mindset, mood, motivation, and hope. After being mentally unable to update my CV for 11 months, I received two job offers from the seven interviews I attended in a single week. While anxiety and depression still lingered, I discovered a newfound sense of well-being, free from the negative side effects that had plagued me while taking antidepressants like headaches, nausea, sexual dysfunction, and numbness that are all too common when used in an incorrect way or on the wrong brains.

4 psychotherapists, 3 psychologists, 2 GPs, and 1 Psychiatrist later, I had accumulated diagnoses and additional possibilities of anxiety, depression, obsessive-compulsive disorder, borderline personality disorder, and major depressive disorder. For each one, I cried my eyes out and then went home to do my research. None of them made enough sense and none of them clicked until I read into ADHD in women (specifically) which I'll admit, I never realised is one of the very few conditions that presents differently in men and women.

As I persevered through the Irish healthcare system (having to go exclusively private), at 26 years old I compiled a list of 75 symptoms that resonated with my childhood experiences and present struggles.

Finally confirming my combined type ADHD diagnosis shed light on the true nature of my challenges, finally dispelling the self-deprecating joke I always made about having a "paradoxical personality." I was and am still desperate to "fulfil my potential" and after using both stimulant medication and psychedelics, I can confirm that both have their benefits despite targeting different mechanisms in the brain. Even though I had made significant improvements in self-medicating with mushrooms. None of the professionals I dealt with had the freedom to engage in that conversation with me and learn from my first-hand experience, which I believe is a total shame for the patients who don't want to take the pharmaceutical route. Surviving 26 years with undiagnosed ADHD stands as one of my greatest personal accomplishments. However, it's unfortunate that I cannot include it on my CV as such. Yet, why wouldn't an employer value someone who has demonstrated resilience, integrity, courage, and independence throughout their career journey? Someone open about their strengths and weaknesses, willing to discuss them in an interview, and possesses self-awareness, empathy, innovation, and entrepreneurial spirit? The stereotypes associated with ADHD are frustrating, as they are always extremely negative and do not include any of our endless superpowers.

Imagine informing your manager about your ADHD diagnosis and the need for regular doctor's appointments to level up your ability to be a productive human. Instead of understanding or asking questions, your manager requests proof and implies that something must be seriously wrong if I need an hour off work every fortnight. Why yes miss, my brain isn't working, would you say that if I had a heart condition? After months of bullying and threats, I decided that Irish society is not ready to support neurodivergent people on a professional level and I also wasn't willing to pretend that I had a neurotypical brain like them, Because I don't, and I will never want one.

Shortly after, I followed my spontaneous nature to find more novel experiences on my own in Southeast Asia. I continue to dig deep every day in order to learn more about myself and the people I meet along the way. Whilst I've been seen all my life as ditsy and aloof, disorganised, and forgetful - I am also wildly brave and independent and despite the struggles, I have every day, I am resilient and that, in and of itself, is enough.

Kema Morrin's Story

As a neurodivergent person, I feel and sense my way through life. I can feel it when something isn't being said. I can sense when a person is lying. I have sensitivities to sound, light, people, food, and smells. I feel pain on a deep level. I'm so used to feeling that I'm not 'good enough', I've done something 'wrong' or be 'too much', that I experience self-loathing often. I trust very few people because I've learned that it's safer to rely on myself than to be let down by people, I thought I could trust. I am unable to tolerate bullshit. I get frustrated fast. I can only do one thing at a time, or I get overwhelmed. I need downtime with nothingness to recover from the exhaustion of the day. Sometimes I ask myself 'Why can't I just be normal?'...

I grew up the life and soul of the party. I wasn't conscious of any of this at the time, but I regularly numbed out the pain and dysfunction of life through any substance that would distract me from it. My breakdown (or breakthrough) woke me from a deep hypnotic state. It was the catalyst for me to realise I was operating in a world that expected me to be something and someone I am not. The disconnection was real, and my body knew it. My breakdown allowed me to go inward and reflect on what I actually needed, and even if I didn't have the answers, I was beginning to realise what was no longer working for me, and that major things in my life needed to change. I came to realise we live in a dualistic world. North pole and South pole, like and dislike, love, and hate, black and white. I believe in this life, there is grey, and cultivating non-duality is how we create the world we want to live in. In a world where hate is met with hate, we are not coming into balance, harmony, and coherence. We cannot continue to choose to put our energy into 'us' and 'them'. It creates more division and judgement in an already highly divided and judgemental society. As neurodivergent people, if we want equality, respect, and compassion, we must happily and openly give those things to ourselves and others.

As I write now, I have undiagnosed ADHD. I am comfortable with not getting diagnosed. However, I am currently moving through a stage in my life where my hormones are changing due to perimenopause, and this has made my experience of ADHD much more prevalent, which is something I know affects many people. I'm open to changing my mind about going through the diagnostic process, but for now, I don't have the desire to deal with a disheartening healthcare system that doesn't serve me.

There are so many more people realising they are neurodivergent now. I'm not fully sure of the reasons why, but I believe it's part of our conscious awakening out of the old ways that serve only some people, and into new ways that serve all. I believe that we can be a part of that shift. The neurodiverse movement is here. We belong. We are all here to teach compassion and understanding, love and acceptance. Not everybody's brain operates the same way. It's time to include this community and create systems that support us so that we can thrive.

My silver lining: I am it. I am my silver lining. Have you ever heard of the expression 'away with the fairies?' Well, that's how I want to live. Day in, day out. In tune with nature, responding to the natural nudge of where to go and what to do next, not getting bogged down by the busyness and distractions of life, just being.

Can you imagine a life where you make the rules? This is the life I strive for. Cultivating my own sense of belonging, one that isn't force-fed to me through a patriarchal, inverted education and work system. I choose my reality. I do this by understanding my human complexity, and knowing how I navigate this world so that I can best support myself (this is an ongoing process of realisation and learning). I have yet to meet a neurodivergent person who hasn't gone deep into their own psyche to gain more of an understanding of themselves. People that know themselves more deeply can be of better service in this world, to themselves and others. If we dare to be authentic then I believe we can lead the world into new, more inclusive ways. But it's not just about the future, it's also about who we are now as individuals and what we can contribute to creating a world that is inclusive of all.

Sarah O' M's Story

Retrospect

I've learned not to go through memories with others as most people just dismiss it, as just "kid stuff, teen stuff, imposter syndrome, parent stuff...Sure we're all like that". When you meet someone who knows though, you know they know and you both "get it".

Re-telling or re-framing childhood isn't a sob story, or exposé. There was nothing different, I was normal, sweet, good to have around my parents' friends; mannerly, chatty.

Childhood - part 1

But it didn't work too well in a school playground or with peers, I was not at ease with peers.

Well, that was my memory, my experience, my lingering memories that then carved out a way of being and feeling and experiencing the world and those around me. Like everything, others would just dismiss this.

This informed poor decisions on my part and was mostly to the detriment of my mental health. Once again, others would dismiss this. This may not be what others perceived of my life. Isn't that what makes it such a challenge? The world seems to know me better than me.

I'm nearly 50, and whatever "ways" I had that might have been less palatable as a child were knocked out or fine-chiselled out with elocution lessons, extra study, good posture, correct diction, obedience, respect, fear, fitting in. I'd swing from being the most endearing, compliant "thing" to meltdown mode.

I probably protected myself by steering away from social activities with other kids, I felt very uncomfortable in most situations with others that felt "unsafe" - boys, and people older than me.

Overall, there was a general paranoia that people would:

-laugh at me

-think I was fat, (I hated how my legs looked and

felt when I crossed them- the fatness - having researched autism to death I think it described as proprioception),

-Think I was "posh" and possibly spoke "too well" with some verbosity and grandiose (much to the delights of my mum),

-think I overate. I was conscious of my appetite, (once again, through research understanding interoception. has explained this), but there was no communication from the brain to the stomach. I clearly remember my insatiable appetite coming in from school, followed by the nausea of having overeaten. The hunger wasn't helped by the utter self-consciousness around food at lunchtime, in fact, I generally asked if I could leave to go to my dad's bar (which was beside the school) during lunch break as I wouldn't want to eat with others, plus I'd very particular preferences and sensitive tastebuds to texture so school lunches didn't work. (I turned vegetarian ca 11yo).

-think I was no fun to play with, always the last to

be chosen

All of the above isn't meant to suggest an eating disorder but it explains my relationship with my body and food.

My mum brought me to a dressmaker to get clothes made for me (still not fully sure why) ... I think it was a combination of clothes not fitting (I wasn't very big, but pudgy), plus I think the fabrics bothered me too.

I felt more accepted by my parent's friends. A secondary school teacher referred to me sarcastically "You think you're an old sage" Another nun warned my mum that I was outspoken/transparent with what I said to others. I was clumsy, breaking the good china. I remember walking like a toy soldier through China shops so that I wouldn't knock stuff over. I don't know if this was normal.

The smell of other children's breath, and their BO, combined with just not feeling accepted made primary school not hugely pleasant.

Post-diagnosis and understanding how I was and ultimately identifying as autistic puts all of the above into context.

Observations- part 1

I think there is cynicism around the outpouring of neurodiverse diagnoses, but if it helps little children or more importantly helps the parents of little kids understand and just accept them for what they are and work with them, then society and adult mental health services may benefit in 30 years.

Teenage me - part 1

The above led to a haphazard chaotic teen, others say "Sure I was like that". In a neurotypical way they could be, but how I experienced life as a teen was quite awful.

My daughter - part 1

Probably what triggered it in my daughter is similar to me. I was unaware of this world for the first 46 years of my life and the first 14 years of her life. I know that unknown to myself, the way I was as a parent has impacted her mental health. I'm not "blaming" myself. Her older brother responded fine, but the combination of how my daughter is, how I am, how I was, and a myriad of other factors has brought us here. But I know that how I parented her wasn't what a little girl like Isobel needed.

Twenty-something

I survived the teens and moved to college where I could prove myself. Split Sarah arrived, I embraced study, but I'd swing from safe to scary.

I met a guy too young when I was in college, 30 years ago, a great guy. We're still married but if I had financial independence I would walk away. I can see how we stayed together, if I'd had more insights into me, I'd have been able to see what was right/wrong. I feel quite passionate about this, as I don't want my daughter to fall into the same situation. He's a great guy, but our relationship isn't good for my mental health, we've tried different supports. Once again, the world won't accept this, he thinks 'I'm mad', 'it's the trauma of mental health issues at home', but like always no one is trusting my instincts. I have nothing to benefit from by separating.

Mental health issues are sometimes a description of embracing a person's neurodiversity. I don't believe this needs to happen with ASD or ADHD. A by-product of not understanding oneself or being understood prompts mental health issues.

My son and daughter both have ADHD, and my daughter has ASD too.

I can't parent them as a neurotypical parent, part of my NT parenting created an eating disorder, depression, suicidality, substance abuse, and no school for 3 years. The trauma.

Thirty-something

Babies, babies. Stay-at-home mum, working mum. Disconnected from babies, I kept having them despite severe Hyperemesis. I read the parenting books; it didn't seem to work. Anything that we perceived as having worked, has subsequently come back to haunt us, the idea of what "I should do", the "kids should do". I always felt overwhelmed but appeared like I had it sorted. No one: partner, In-laws, GP, friends - no one accepted my fears.

The relationship with the daughter was getting worse, it felt wrong. No one was listening and it made little sense. My husband couldn't relate to my version of life, for him it was largely 'tickety boo'. It was good enough.

Moods swung and fall. Usual relationship rows. Physically it didn't feel right either. But I had no other experience of a relationship.

40 - mid 40's the idea of self-preservation came into my vocabulary... I wasn't happy, my daughter sensed this. She wasn't happy - teen tantrums and chaos. Sulky, disenfranchised. She said once 'If you could be happy, I'd be happy'. That was very revealing.

Then the ADHD/ASD journey began with my daughter. Before this neurodivergence, neurotypical, neurodivergent hadn't occupied any headspace.

I know the world is trying to get its head around all of this. It has always been there unrecognised, those sad stories of suicide and chronic depression and those who were 'weird' or just didn't fit in. For that reason, I think the heightened awareness of ND might help us.

Below are some other notes I had drafted and sent to a group seeking feedback from the adult autistic community on a document" Guideline for Counsellors and Psychotherapists to Work in a Neuro-affirmative Way with Autistic Adult Clients" and are seeking feedback?

The idea behind the document would be to inform the work practices of counsellors and psychotherapists and help contribute to a training plan for all IACP Therapists.

This is possibly written better!

From the few years I have been involved with counsellors and therapists many include the 'neuro affirmative approach' on their websites, and list it as a specialisation but in my experience, it has not translated into an environment which actually listens to the autistic voice and supports their experience.

It seems to sway from

- not believing or accepting the autistic diagnosis, on the basis that someone appears to be articulate or 'functioning' – that 'we all have a bit of that'.
- Massive scepticism around more acronyms. It can feel like they think it's an 'on-trend' movement.
- Then, when there is acceptance a lack of understanding of what the experience actually is.
- Sometimes deep-rooted PTSD experiences from childhood, which may appear innocuous to others aren't given the space needed, once again 'sure that's the way it was back then'.

Prior to diagnosis, I didn't even know that there was a 'more true' version of myself, more authentic. I just didn't. Given the explosion and awareness of mental health, another recommendation is that psychotherapists/counsellors form part of the GP team and would ideally be treated as GP services (like a nurse) from a Private Health Insurance point of view which has very poor cover for therapy. The 'medical model' as captured in the document can worsen the autistic's experience, I would have spoken to my GP for over 10 years about issues, and at every visit, it was dismissed that we're all struggling with kids, partners, work etc… Even when suicidal thoughts were mentioned. After 10 years, either antidepressants or counselling was finally suggested, but with little guidance on this. The relevance is that any thoughts on this were dismissed both by those around me and by my GP. This had an impact on me and my children as I kept doing what I did, which followed 'parenting' approaches taught by and to neurotypical parents.

The impact of this has been significant as the world crumbled around us three years ago with my daughter: SH, ED in all its forms, Depression, suicidality, she has hardly attended school in 3 years, now drugs and very high-risk activity.

Impulsivity, compulsivity, addiction, and the need for utter control. Classic ASD and ADHD.

Laura G. A.

Two years ago, a brilliant Psychiatrist in Crumlin suggested that my daughter might be autistic. This was a lightbulb moment, for which I will always be indebted. 18 months later and after constant battles with psychiatrists, psychologists, psychotherapists, and senior Mental Health professionals her autistic self was finally recognized (as was mine). During this time CAMHS also diagnosed her as having ADHD.

The surprising thing was that psychotherapists also refused to take on board what I knew was the truth and what I had experienced with her as a younger child.

When these aspects aren't taken on board by therapists it slows down the restorative therapeutic process in terms of how they communicate and engage with the autistic person to support them. When therapists ignore these needs and try to support them through conventional ways e.g., CBT etc... it could cause more damage as the autistic person might not be able to respond to this, which makes us feel even worse and more stupid.

Feeling stupid, 'outraged, emotionally dysregulated, inconsistent parent, insecure, hormonal, menopausal, at times suicidal woman, not knowing if she should be on anti-depressants, or she was just a crap person'.

Psychotherapists and professionals do not want to recognize their 'functioning patients' as being autistic.

Learning about how my autistic-self, experienced the world opened a new version of the world to me. It hasn't 'fixed' anything (I don't want it to), but it has helped so much.

There is also the feeling that medical professionals still disbelieve and view a late diagnosis as a 'midlife crisis', a convenient escape route.

It can also be weaponized.

I heard one psychotherapist mention that the ND movement is taking over, and the MH of NT is not being taken into consideration.

This questioning erodes any self-validation that an

autistic person works on (through psychotherapy) as it continually feels like it is invalidation: issues such as 'emotional dysregulation, black and white thinking, and inflexibility are described as being the fault of being autistic.

A diagnosis

- Helps make sense of the past

  - Misdiagnosis can be a barrier to authentic autistic growth

  - It is not a mental illness, but not understanding the innate predispositions that make us up results in MH issues

- Not accepted, misunderstood

  - Experience of food – a– very slow to pick up on an underlying understanding of autism, this seriously hinders the support that the person needs.

  - NT are less accurate at interpreting the mental state of autistics, misdiagnosis or overlooking suicidal ideation.

- A diagnosis also makes sense of the:

  o relationships formed (marital) and the poor communication (some detrimental) in them.

o Bad employment choices can also have a massive impact on MH

o Challenges with Parenting – unpredictable, overwhelming, need for strong bonds with kids – which (in my case) has had massive ramifications.

- The biggest issue is being misunderstood by others.

- The personal relationship between client and therapist must be mutual, two-way, and authentic.

Two years into psychotherapy I have found the psychotherapist helpful, but I think I have educated him (though haven't quite sought that affirmation)

Sivan Hong's Story @ sivan_hong_author

We all come to ADHD in our own ways. For me, my discovery didn't come through typical routes, it wasn't a result of struggling in school or work (even though looking back now, those challenges should have made my diagnosis very apparent). I found my way to this diagnosis at the age of 47, through the experiences of my beautiful, ADHD children.

Their diagnosis was like a mirror, reflecting not just their reality, but also mine. And suddenly, our family portrait had a new shade - we were different, journeying through a world of neurotypical norms.

As an author, I find words to be powerful.

They define our world, shape our perceptions, and express our deepest emotions. They are like a secret club that if we could understand them, it could transform our reality. As a newly minted member of the ADHD club, I found myself lost in the sea of terms and emotions. How could I have this new identity? What happened to my old one? I went through a period of mourning for who I thought I was, and I was angry for not knowing sooner. And like so many of us, I could not stop Googling. I came across so many terms and so many experiences. Some of them fit but others did not. But in this craziness of new terms and emotions, one term reached out and really fit - neurodiversity.

Neurodiversity. This term took me out of the shock of a diagnosis and helped me in my understanding of ADHD. Rooted in science, it encompasses all brain and learning differences - Autism, ADHD, Dyslexia, and more. It was there to tell me that even though parts of ADHD were hard, there was not something "wrong" with me. It told me and the world that our brains were not malfunctioning or deficient. They were different, a unique blend of chaos and creativity. It was not about deficits; it was about differences. I could work with differences. And these differences brought incredible strengths with them.

This understanding was a lifeline for me, as a

mother, and as a woman grappling with a late-life ADHD diagnosis. It was like the world suddenly clicked into place, like a puzzle piece finding its home. My brain wasn't faulty or broken; it was just different, and in that difference, it was beautifully unique. And so were my children's brains.

As a mom, I had to make sure that my boys grew up understanding this truth. I needed them to realize that they weren't damaged goods but beautiful minds with incredible capabilities. They had to see that their difference was not a curse, but a superpower, their superpower. But the journey of teaching this to my kids was not without challenges.

One such challenge was finding appropriate resources to communicate this truth to them. As an advocate of storytelling, I embarked on a quest to find picture books that showcased neurodiverse characters, characters that mirrored my boys. But this quest was harder than I thought. The few books I found either trivialized or dramatized the differences, creating caricatures instead of characters. My boys needed to see characters who loved their routines, who needed breaks from the chaos of life, who found solace in fidget toys or comfort in chewing gum. They needed to see their experiences reflected, normalized, and celebrated. And then, in the most unexpected turn of events, I found a new calling. Seeing the void in children's literature, I took it upon myself to fill it. I took on the hat of an author and illustrator to tell the stories that were missing. And thus, the Super Fun Day Books series was born, a collection of stories about neurodiverse children, like mine, navigating life's twists and turns.

These books are not just stories. They are guides, fashioned after social stories used in special education, with an intentional focus on making them accessible to everyone. With simplistic illustrations to maintain focus on the narrative and a dyslexic-friendly font, my goal was to make these stories reachable and relatable to all children, not just those with ADHD.

Our journey with neurodiversity is like a

rollercoaster ride, full of highs and lows. There are days when my boys celebrate their uniqueness, and there are days when they yearn for 'normalcy'. My books serve as a reminder to me on these tumultuous days, encouraging them to embrace their unique brain-wiring.

But my books are not just for neurodiverse children or their parents. They are windows into our world for neurotypical children. By introducing them to the joys and challenges of neurodiversity, these stories foster empathy and understanding. They create a dialogue about our differences and similarities. Because, as much as I can shape my children's perception of themselves, it's equally important that their environment reflects the same acceptance and appreciation for diversity.

As women with ADHD, we often feel like we're swimming upstream in a world that wasn't designed for us. But remember, it's in these uncharted waters that we discover our strength, our resilience. As we learn to embrace our unique brains, we teach our children to do the same. So, let's continue to ride this wild wave of neurodiversity together, for ourselves and our little ones. Let's shape a world that sees, accepts, and celebrates every kind of brain.

By Sivan Hong

Proud member of the ADHD community, mother of neurodivergent kids and children's book author.

Steve's Story

My name is Steve, I'm 37 and I'm from Essex in the UK.

How do I keep this short while explaining enough? Let's see.

In terms of ADHD and starting from the beginning, I was "diagnosed" at around age 9, I was being assessed in a clinic for my struggles at school. I was diagnosed with Dyscalculia, and I had a pink plastic card to lay over the paper to read better because they suspected I might have dyslexia, although it turned out I just needed better glasses and had to stop lying to my optician about how my eyesight was. Anyway, the clinician who was assessing me handed my mum a leaflet and said, (and I'm paraphrasing here) Something along the lines of "I think your son has ADHD, take this and you might find it useful".

And that's where it began really. Everything my mom went on to learn about ADHD just showed that I was a poster boy for it and my family have accepted that's what it is ever since. So that was my informal diagnosis. This was the 90s, so we didn't know much about it, and this was the first we had ever heard of ADHD. In fact, we weren't alone.

I got no help with ADHD as a kid and in school and because it is such a complex disorder, it's very difficult to distinguish the difference between ADHD struggles (in school and learning) and general age academic struggles and there was an uneven balance of understanding between my family at my teachers. So, it was tough for me to understand too. When you are constantly asked why can't you learn to like the other kids? By your teachers, you question yourself and here begins a world of problems.

Imposter syndrome

The teacher says I should be able to sit still and listen.

RSD

Been told that I'm not doing good enough. Self-doubt

I can't do this. Everyone else makes this look easy (sitting still and paying attention).

So, I stood out in school. I was different from the other kids. The plus side to all this is that it's never bothered me. Blissfully unaware of what I was at school to do, I just treated it like a youth club. I liked standing out. I liked being different. I think I knew then although I can't say for sure, but I do know now, it was never a matter of intelligence. I knew I wasn't stupid, but I couldn't explain to anyone how bored I was with the structure of school.

So, let's fast forward. I have always been active. What I didn't know then was how much being active was keeping some ADHD symptoms under control. The exercise I was getting was my only real form of self-medicating. Climbing trees, running around exploring and just generally being an outdoorsy adventure-seeking kid. Then I found skateboarding and have carried this on into adulthood. From age 9 when I started to about age 27-28, I would go skateboarding almost every day. I've always had hobbies that not only supply my dopamine but that also would regulate me in terms of ADHD symptom control.

A physical job and a physical lifestyle meant that the only things that ever showed up were fidgeting, the odd violent mood swings and some extreme emotional dysregulation.

Then I became apparent and basically, shit hit the fan.

Every little type of self-regulating, self-medicating strategy I had built for myself over all these years that kept me in check came to an abrupt end. I couldn't do any of the things I used to do in what I can only now see as a selfish way of living because life was no longer all about me. My focus had shifted to my baby and all my own needs were put aside.

If this makes me sound like an awful person, then it's only because I'm not very good at explaining.

I chose to be a parent. It's a life goal of mine to raise children and be the best dad I can be! If I can be half as good as my parents have been and are today, I'll be doing great. What I didn't allow for was the change of life that I was used to and hadn't realised until becoming a dad, had kept ADHD in the background.

So now I'm out of control. The things I would do to keep everything running smoothly had gone. My sleep pattern and how much-unbroken sleep I got. Gone. The food I was eating and at regular times of the day. Gone. The downtime I allow myself if I ever feel overwhelmed or emotional. Gone. The list goes on.

I hadn't thought at the time that I should try and keep doing all these things because it was working for me, so it wasn't until it all stopped, and the cracks began to show that I realized it was.

I was so focused on caring for my baby that I dropped everything I had been doing. That and the fact that I no longer had free and flexible time to do any of it well being a new dad.

Anyway. It got pretty bad. I was back to being the poster boy for ADHD and I couldn't find the time to get a structure built for myself again to manage it. My working memory just doesn't work at all, and I started to feel like I wasn't being the best dad I could be. I couldn't remember to do important things and my emotions were all over the place.

Then one day my baby girl fell down the stairs because I forgot to shut the gate. Luckily, she was fine, but I was devastated. I broke down in tears that night talking to my wife and told her I wanted help.

I had never considered medication before to treat ADHD and because of this point, I was 35-ish and had lived with it all my life so far. It was normal to me. I also never considered myself to have a brain that was different to anyone else's. But I needed help, so I called health in mind.

I said I was calling because I wanted to know if I could try ADHD meds in the hope, they couldn't prove my memory. Something I had read that said they can support better working memory. That and the emotional outbursts that were the main problem. We spoke on the phone for a couple of hours, and she agreed I wasn't depressed and understood my reasons for calling. She managed to bypass my GP with an email requesting my referral for a diagnosis of ADHD and that's what I got.

I was diagnosed and started titration on xaggitin XL and booked in for eight hours of ADHD coaching.

While all of this was going on, I learned old and new ways in which two better manage it and then I stopped taking the med after just shy of a year.

Then I decided I would start an Instagram account sharing all of this and my insights on ADHD and all of its highs and lows in an attempt to help raise awareness.

ADHD is debilitating and it is no joke. It's not cool or trendy to want to have it but it's important to those who do have it to know that life can be good and happy and successful with it too. I am now blessed with some knowledge and coping skills that allow me to thrive and understand that I have my battles for a reason. If I can help in any way to get people aware of it and understand it better, that is the least I can do.

Elise Cordaro's Story @audhd_bestie

I always knew I was different from my peers. And although the signs were there, my parents, teachers and I never thought about autism or ADHD because back then we knew too little about it.

For example, as a child, I was already a very bad sleeper. Of course, this is common in children. But my sleeping issues were different. As a baby, I slept all day and was awake all night. I think this was a case of severe delayed sleep phase syndrome which is common among people with ADHD. I was also scared of balloons, because they could explode, and the bang hurt my ears.

But the clearest sign was my inability to concentrate in school. From the age of 5, until I finished my master's degree at the age of 25, school was an ordeal. But my grades were good, so nobody looked any further. And I didn't talk about it because I was ashamed. I thought I was a 'bad' child for not being able to focus and for losing so much time staring out of the window. I taught myself to make time schedules and I managed to find all sorts of coping mechanisms to get my degrees. I also developed my study method; bottom-up instead of the neurotypical top-down.

It was only around the age of 19 that I seriously started to consider that my differences were not just my character, but that there had to be more. A condition. A diagnosis. I was feeling more and more down and when my parents divorced, I realized that the way I reacted to it was just weird. So, I started researching and I turned to Dr. Google. But because I had no clue that a lot of my particular traits were actually symptoms, I didn't have all the pieces of the puzzle.

I consulted a couple of psychologists, but they weren't any help. During my search for what was 'wrong' with me, a fellow student spoke to me about ADHD and the trouble to focus. Immediately a light bulb went on in my head. Not being able to focus could be a symptom. Maybe it's not my fault? Maybe ADHD is the answer?

I did some research about ADHD and could hardly believe it. This is me! Finally! After all these years, I found the answer! At the time, I had just done a couple of sessions with a new psychologist and decided to share my findings with her at the next session. She reacted in a very irritated way and said it was impossible because I had a master's degree. 'There is nothing wrong with you', she said.

Her reaction made me feel that I was fussing and exaggerating. That I just needed to toughen up. Because of this, it took me another 6 months before I decided to go to a psychiatrist to start an assessment to find out whether I had ADHD or not. The results were clear: I had ADHD. At that time, I was 26. A year later I was also diagnosed with autism, so I was 27. Between the start of my search and the answer to my question were 8 long years... At that time, I was already working full-time and living on my own. And that was a lot harder than I had imagined. But thanks to my diagnoses, I understood why adult life was so demanding.

After my diagnoses, I started to develop better

coping mechanisms to deal with daily life and I started a blog where I shared my tips and tricks. A couple of years later, I wrote my first book. It's in Dutch. But after almost 4 years it will be translated into English! The title will be: 'Thriving Differently. How I navigate life with autism and ADHD'.

Today I don't work full-time anymore. After 6 years, I started working 4 days instead of 5 and 2 years later I decided to work only 3 days. It's not easy financially but it was necessary.

Because the most difficult about autism and ADHD to live with for me personally is fatigue. I'm extremely tired. All. The. Time. Life is so draining. So, I had no choice but to work less. A couple of months ago, I started a side hustle to compensate financially. I made my own planner and I'm selling it through my web shop.

I hope to be able to leave my 9 to 5 job one day and to be able to live from my own business so that I can live life on my own terms.

Roxanne's Story @adhdletstalk

Two years after having my first child I was scrolling social media and started making a joke with my husband that "I probably had ADHD". Only the more I read, the less of a joke it became... I was an adult woman, I wasn't hyperactive, I did well in school, I didn't know ADHD was an option for me, yet here it was in black and white- an exclamation for most of my struggles, were what I had simply took as my slightly weird, OTT personality. My clumsiness, slightly social awkwardness often always saying what was on my mind, my people pleasing tendencies, distractibility, emotional dysregulation, high sensitivity to rejection, constant nail biting, rocking, losing things all the time, impulsivity, racing thoughts... However, it wasn't until after having a child, things got immensely harder- my mental health tanked and I thought Post Natal Depression was to blame - now I know it was my undiagnosed ADHD roaring to the surface.

At my point of diagnosis, I had two children and as I

deep dove into anything at everything ADHD, i was left feeling more and more annoyed that so little was known about this condition in anybody other than CIS men/ boys. So, in the space of about two months I found a course I could undertake that allowed me to be able to do my own research into this topic, I interviewed for it and got accepted.

And it's been a bit of a whirlwind since then. I am so passionate about diversifying the research, and understanding more about ADHD and how it affects a wider range of people. I think people's voices and stories need to be at the forefront of this. What better way to understand someone's experience, than by hearing it directly from them?

That casual joke I made a year ago has took me on a bit of a journey, and I am constantly worried my interest/focus will wane or I will get a crisis of confidence and stop before I get rejected (as has often happened before with other projects), but while it is still there I am taking that drive and hopefully turning it into something useful.

AuDHD & Me

When I created my Instagram page ADHDletstalk I wanted this space to be a space of validation, normalization, inclusive, representative, destigmatizing, myth busting, shame free and most importantly, a whole variety of voices and stories. So, if that space you want to be involved in-let's talk you will find me on my Instagram page @ADHDletstalk

Epilogue

This is by no means the end of my story; it's just the beginning. This was an amazing, tear-filled, fun, and horrifying journey. And I loved every bit of it. I hope it started something with you, the reader. Maybe it gave you the oomph needed to check out that diagnosis you've been putting off.

I enjoyed writing this book, but I must admit it was not all easy. I struggled looking back at my relationships, when I was reading and editing this chapter the other day, I got very low. I have some unresolved trauma about this. I also need to get a hang on the expectations and wants of others and what I need and want. On a lighter side, I know how lucky and happy I am to be with my husband, a person who understands me and is my confidante and, I can just be me. He is truly my best friend, and he has helped me so much and is the main reason for me to stop and consider my own needs. But I do have a lot of to work on. There is so much I never allowed to come up, I feel it bubbling under the surface.

Update on medication, I am still on Tvense and up to 50mg. The effects have been incredible: I am more aware of my emotional state and how I am feeling. My son has noticed the difference too. He is very sensitive to my emotional state, and he had been a little testy the last few weeks. However, that has also greatly improved, which may or may not be a link but is notable. In addition, with the 50mg, I am much calmer. I am still very alert and clear-headed, but calmer. With the lower dosages, I tended to jump to new tasks, while my mind was a lot more organised (which was my priority). On the other hand, I can also move when I'm needed, such as when my son calls me, and I can even return to work immediately. Furthermore, sleep has been consistently good the last few weeks. I am relaxing in the evenings now, while I am working later to get my thesis chapter done.

If you want to talk about anything from the book, or chat my Instagram page is _audhd_and_me_

Laura G. A.

Biography

American Psychiatric Association: Diagnostic and statistical manual of mental disorders. Washington: American Psychiatric Publishing, Fifth Edition, 2013.

Ashinoff, B.K. & Abu-Akel, A. 2021. Hyperfocus: the forgotten frontier of attention. Psychol Res. 85(1),1-19. doi: 10.1007/s00426-019-01245-8. PMID: 31541305; PMCID: PMC7851038.

Barnes, J., Binnie, L. & Blakemore, S. J. 2023. The effects of emotional literacy training on neurodivergent students in mainstream schools: A randomized controlled trial. Journal of Autism and Developmental Disorders, 53(1), 123-135. https://doi.org/10.1007/s10803-022-05277-8

Baron-Cohen, S., Johnson, D., Asher, J., Wheelwright, S., Fisher, S.E., Gregersen, P.K. & Allison, C. 2013. Is synaesthesia more common in autism? Molecular Autism, 4, 1–6. doi: 10.1186/2040-2392-4-40.

Baron-Cohen, S., Robson, E., Lai, M.C. & Allison, C. 2016. Mirror-Touch Synaesthesia Is Not Associated with Heightened Empathy, and Can Occur with Autism. PLoS One. 11(8): e0160543. doi: 10.1371/journal.pone.0160543. PMID: 27490947; PMCID: PMC4973977.

Bijlenga D, Tjon-Ka-Jie JYM, Schuijers F, Kooij JJS. Atypical sensory profiles as core features of adult ADHD, irrespective of autistic symptoms. Eur Psychiatry. 43, 51-57. doi: 10.1016/j.eurpsy.2017.02.481. PMID: 28371743.

Cage E, Troxell-Whitman Z. 2019. Understanding the Reasons, Contexts and Costs of Camouflaging for Autistic Adults. J Autism Dev Disord. 49(5):1899-1911. doi: 10.1007/s10803-018-03878-x. PMID: 30627892; PMCID: PMC6483965.

Cazalis, F., Reyes E., Leduc, S. & Gourion, D. 2022. Evidence That Nine Autistic Women Out of Ten Have Been Victims of Sexual Violence. Frontiers in Behavioral Neuroscience, 16.

Deweerdt, S. 2020. Repetitive behaviors and 'stimming' in autism, explained. Spectrum.https://doi.org/10.53053/ERTG7729

de Giambattista Concetta, Ventura, P., Trerotoli P., Margari F. & Margari L. 2021. Sex Differences in Autism Spectrum Disorder: Focus on High Functioning Children and Adolescents. Frontiers in Psychiatry, 12.

Gillberg, G. 1990. What is Autism? International Review of Psychiatry, 2 (1), 61-66, DOI: 10.3109/09540269009028272.

Green, J., Absoud, M., Grahame, V., Malik, O., Simonoff, E., Frcpch, A. & Baird, G. 2018. Pathological Demand Avoidance: symptoms but not a syndrome. The Lancet Child & Adolescent Health. 2. 10.1016/S2352-4642(18)30044-0.

Gruson-Wood, J. 2016. Autism, Expert Discourses, and Subjectification: A Critical Examination of Applied Behavioural Therapies. Studies in Social Justice. 10. 38-58. 10.26522/ssj.v10i1.1331.

Hendricks, D. 2010. Employment and adults with autism spectrum disorders: Challenges and strategies for success Journal of Vocational Rehabilitation. 32, 125–134 DOI:10.3233/JVR-

Hudson, C.C., Hall, L. & Harkness, K.L. 2019. Prevalence of Depressive Disorders in Individuals with Autism Spectrum Disorder: A H ADHD. Front Integr Neurosci. 13, 40. doi: 10.3389/fnint.2019.00040. PMID: 31555103; PMCID: PMC6742721.

Laura G. A.

Hurlbutt, K., & Chalmers, L. 2004. Employment and Adults with Asperger Syndrome. Focus on Autism and Other Developmental Disabilities, 19(4), 215–222. https://doi.org/10.1177/10883576040190040301

Katzman, M.A., Bilkey, T.S., Chokka, P.R., Fallu, A. & Klassen, L.J. 2017. Adult ADHD and comorbid disorders: clinical implications of a dimensional approach. BMC Psychiatry. 17, 302. doi: 10.1186/s12888-017-1463-3. PMID: 28830387; PMCID: PMC5567978.

Leitner, Y. 2014. The Co-Occurrence of Autism and Attention Deficit Hyperactivity Disorder in Children - What Do We Know? Frontiers in human neuroscience. 8. 268. 10.3389/fnhum.2014.00268.

van Leeuwen T.M., Neufeld, J., Hughes, J. & Ward, J. 2020. Synaesthesia and autism: Different developmental outcomes from overlapping mechanisms? Cognitive Neuropsychology. 37(7-8), 433-449. doi: 10.1080/02643294.2020.1808455. PMID: 32845799.

Maslach, C. & Leiter, M.P. 2016. Understanding the burnout experience: recent research and its implications for psychiatry. World Psychiatry. 15(2),103–111. doi:10.1002/wps.20311.

Montazeri, F., de Bildt, A., Dekker, V. & Anderson, G.M. 2020. Network Analysis of Behaviors in the Depression and Autism Realms: Inter-Relationships and Clinical Implications. J Autism Dev Disord., 50(5), 1580-1595. doi: 10.1007/s10803-019-03914-4. PMID: 30778821.

Müller, E.A. & Schuler, A., Burton, B.A. & Yates, Gregory. (2003). Meeting the vocational support needs of individuals with Asperger Syndrome and other autism spectrum disabilities. Journal of Vocational Rehabilitation. 18, 163-175.

Neufeld, J., Roy, M., Zapf, A., Sinke, C., Emrich, H.M., Prox-Vagedes, V. & Zedler, M. 2013. Is synaesthesia more common in patients with Asperger syndrome? Frontiers in Human Neuroscience

Raymaker, D.M., Teo, A.R., Steckler, N.A., Lentz, B., Scharer, M., Delos Santos, A., Kapp, S.K., Hunter, M., Joyce, A. & Nicolaidis, C. 2020. Having All of Your Internal Resources Exhausted Beyond Measure and Being Left with No Clean-Up Crew": Defining Autistic Burnout. Autism in Adulthood, 2:2, 132-143

Senju, A. 2012. Spontaneous theory of mind and its absence in autism spectrum disorders. Neuroscientist. 18(2),108-13. doi: 10.1177/1073858410397208. PMID: 21609942; PMCID: PMC3796729.

Sikora, D.M., Vora, P., Coury, D.L. & Rosenberg, D. 2012. Attention-deficit/hyperactivity disorder symptoms, adaptive functioning, and quality of life in children with autism spectrum disorder.130, Suppl 2:S 91-7. doi: 10.1542/peds.2012-0900G. PMID: 23118259.

Simner, J., Mulvenna, C., Sagiv, N., Tsakanikos, E., Witherby, S.A., Fraser, C., Scott, K. & Ward, J. 2006. Synaesthesia: The prevalence of atypical cross-modal experiences.' Perception, 35, 1024-1033.

Skogli, E.W., Teicher, M.H., Andersen, P.N., Hovik, K.T. & Øie M. 2013. ADHD in girls and boys--gender differences in co-existing symptoms and executive function measures. BMC Psychiatry. 9, 13:298. doi: 10.1186/1471-244X-13-298. PMID: 24206839; PMCID: PMC3827008.

Vora P. & Sikora D. 2011. Society for Developmental and Behavioral. San Antonio, TX: Pediatrics

Wood, R. 2019. Autism, intense interests, and support in school: from wasted efforts to shared understandings. Educational Review. 73. 1-21. 10.1080/00131911.2019.1566213.

These are the Instagram pages and youtube channels that helped so much:

Instagram

ADHD_Empowerment_Coaching

Cherry | ADHD Mum on Instagram and TikTok

YouTube

How to ADHD on Youtube

https://www.youtube.com/watch?v=IoJx9sXeP34

https://www.youtube.com/watch?v=uBwGvboe4hM

Neurodiversity in the Workplace: Strategies for Employers and Employees (additudemag.com)

https://www.verywellmind.com/adhd-and-imposter-syndrome-3888166

NOTES

date _____

date _____

date _____

date _____

NOTES

date _____

Printed in Great Britain
by Amazon

44255596R00169